MW01132690

SECOND ASCENT
The Story of HUGH HERR

ALISON OSIUS

STACKPOLE
BOOKS

Published by
STACKPOLE BOOKS
Cameron and Kelker Streets
P.O. Box 1831
Harrisburg, PA 17105

Printed in the United States of America

First Edition

10 9 8 7 6 5 4 3 2 1

Library of Congress Cataloging-in-Publication Data

Osius, Alison.
    Second ascent : the story of Hugh Herr / Alison Osius. – 1st ed.
        p. cm.
    Summary: Describes how a talented rock climber survived a double
amputation at seventeen to return to his chosen sport.
    ISBN 0-8117-1794-1 (HC) : $19.95 ($26.95 in Canada)
    1. Herr, Hugh – Juvenile literature. 2. Mountaineers – United
States – Biography – Juvenile literature. 3. Rock climbing – Juvenile
literature. [1. Herr, Hugh. 2. Mountaineers. 3. Physically
handicapped. 4. Rock climbing.] I. Title.
Gv199.92.H45085   1991
796.5′22′092 – dc20
[B]   91-13171
                                                                        CIP
                                                                        AC

It was Hugh's wish that this book be dedicated to Albert Dow. Although Hugh and I have not always agreed during the making of this book, on this point, we are in perfect accord.

To Albert, who cared

ALBERT DOW

DAVID STONE

PROLOGUE

It was a birthday celebration at the Nereledge Inn in North Conway, New Hampshire, and Hugh Herr had asked everyone to speak of his earliest memory.

At his own turn, Hugh told of how, when he was four years old and all his brothers and sisters were in school, his mother would let him pack up a Boy Scout knapsack. In it he would place a whole box of Raisin Bran, a plastic gallon jug of milk, a big glass bowl, and a cereal spoon. Then he would walk away on his own little expedition.

One sunny day he trundled along for a mile, out in the cornfields. The yellow-green stalks reached higher than he was tall, and he felt small and hidden, like a creature in a story. The ground was crumbly but hard, his feet barely sinking into it, and scattered with round stones and the gray remains of other years' husks and cobs.

Hugh sat down and ate his cereal, then fell asleep. He didn't awake until two hours later.

He stood up. He couldn't see above the green tops of the corn stalks. But he knew he should go back in the direction he had come from, and started home along the trail of his own footprints.

The leaves slap-slapped at his face as he walked between the rows.

One made a small cut on his cheek, like a paper cut, that stung.

At home, his mother had called his father, his brothers, and the neighbors; she sent them all out looking in the woods and fields. They were calling his name when he came walking home.

Now, sixteen years later, Hugh laughed to think of that time. "It's heaven when you're a kid," he said. "There's no danger. The world is for you. You just go out wandering."

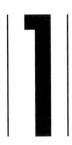

Lancaster, Pennsylvania, is farmland. The landscape is made of dips, swirls, and slopes. Silos and windmills reach upward along the skyline, and by the side of a road a long-bearded farmer in a straw hat may be leading four horses and a wooden plow. All around, the trees are a dozen shades of blue-green, blowing and tossing, many of them six storeys tall and five wide. Piled on each other, they stretch off into the distance, melding into more ridges, more glades, more lines of trees.

Hans Herr settled in Lancaster in 1710. The Herrs were the first nonnatives in the area, and are said to have selected as their home the place where they found the biggest trees.

The Herrs were Mennonites, members of a Christian sect that originated in Switzerland in the sixteenth century as Anabaptists. Considered radicals, they had left the Church of Rome because they believed in the separation of church and state, baptism on confession of faith rather than in infancy, and the church as a free institution with voluntary membership. Their creed forbade joining the military or police force, swearing oaths, or holding offices that required use of force. They believed that Reformation leaders had not accomplished enough.

The Swiss authorities saw the Anabaptists as heretics who could destroy the Roman Catholic church and the state. Anabaptists were chased, burned, beheaded, drowned, and imprisoned by the Reformation church; in Switzerland they were nearly annihilated. Members fled across Europe.

Menno Simons, a Dutch priest, joined the Anabaptist movement in 1536, gathering congregations that came to be known by his name. Dutch Mennonites settled in northern Germany, Prussia, and the Russian Ukraine. The Swiss Mennonites settled mostly in Germany and France; along the Rhine they built terraces and farmed the hillsides but were forbidden to own land. Several thousand of them moved to Pennsylvania when William Penn offered religious liberty and the right of land ownership.

The first Mennonite settlement was in Germantown, Pennsylvania, in 1683, but Lancaster became the New World center for Mennonites and members of a related sect, the Amish, who interpreted the Bible even more strictly. Most settled in rural communities, wanting to be left alone to worship as they chose.

The values of Lancaster-area citizens are rooted in the traditions of the spare, hardworking Amish and Mennonites, known for their plain ways, and their honesty and frugality. They are clean and meticulous, especially the Amish, whose fields, barns, and farmhouses are immaculate. People in Lancaster say that you can tell an Amish farm by looking at it.

Today the Mennonite community is varied. All members have retained their pacifism, but some look and act like the Amish, and others like secular Americans. The Amish continue to believe strongly in the need to remain separate from the world. The women wear long dresses and white prayer caps, the men beards and tall hats; the Amish drive horses and buggies instead of cars, tractors, and other machines. Though less extreme in their appearance and way of life, the Mennonites are plain and conservative. Some women wear prayer caps, but most simply dress modestly and wear little makeup or jewelry. Mennonites are less consistently farmers than the Amish, having gone into the professions.

The descendants of Hans Herr are many. The Lancaster telephone book is filled with Herrs, and signs bearing the name are ubiquitous: the Herr Food Mart, Herr Avenue, E.M. Herr Farm Implements. Herrs have spread all through Lancaster County, to Maryland and Connecticut, south to Florida and off into the western United States. Some have even gone to Australia and other countries.

Farm life remains the foundation of the area. The Central Market in Penn Square, downtown Lancaster, is the country's oldest publicly owned market still in operation. In this dense bazaar of stalls, shoppers buy cheeses, smoked meats, poultry, breads, homemade candy, fruits, flowers, quilts, clocks, and dolls. Amish and Mennonite standholders chat with their neighbors, referred to as the English. From Lancaster come, among other things, cereal, smoked meats, Pennsylvania Dutch Potato Chips, Sturgess Meats, Kitchen Kettle jams and jellies, and pretzels. The population of the city of Lancaster (60,000) and the county (420,000) is growing fast.

John Herr grew up in Lancaster, where his father was a builder and farmer, and his grandfather had had an ice company. At the Eastern Mennonite College in Harrisonburg, Virginia, he met Martha Miller, from a town called Archbold in northwestern Ohio. It was an area of big farms, occupied entirely by close-knit Mennonites who treated each other as a large family. Martha's father started out as a farmer, then became a carpenter, then a cabinetmaker.

John was considered a hellion in college. In a conservative atmosphere, he dressed all in black, as both a prank and a parody of the Mennonite religion. He was dark haired and good looking, a good baseball and basketball player, and a singer with a deep baritone voice. Well after college, at age thirty, he studied opera at the Peabody Conservatory in Baltimore. He was so talented that at age thirty-five he gave a recital at Carnegie Hall.

After he and Martha married, he started his own business as a builder. In addition, he worked the farm, and for eighteen years he put in three hours a day as a chemist. Martha's family had worried about her, hoped that John wouldn't give her children and then run off. Their concerns were ill-founded. He took the business of being a father and husband seriously.

And yet he was flamboyant, with a taste for dramatic entertainment. He would bring the children into his lab, and say, "Watch this!" Then he would drop acid onto a piece of paper. With a *poof* the paper would disintegrate. The children loved the show and the atmosphere, the rows of beakers and bottles, the white coats and cabinets, the bright lights.

Each Christmas Day there was a special ritual. John would run out into the Pennsylvania snow in his underwear. As the children pressed their faces against the window, squealing and shrieking with delight, he would jump into a snowdrift, burst out, and then race back to the house.

"Now, get your father a towel," Martha would say. The children would scramble to the door, clutching a towel for their beaming father.

John's sense of humor sometimes backfired. On one occasion he thought he would startle the children. He picked up a jar of rat poison and said, "Well, this looks good," and put some in his mouth. Suddenly John's eyes widened, and he ran to the bathroom. The agent had dissolved and was burning his tongue. The children were indeed aghast.

Hugh Herr, the fifth and youngest child, was often said to be just like his father—strong willed, and a risk taker. But his more immediate role models were his older brothers, Hans and especially Tony, six years older and always the leader among the three. At the age of four, Hugh took up drawing because Tony was filling a sketchbook.

When Hugh turned four, five-year-old Hans went off to school with Tony and their two sisters, Beth and Ellen, who were four and five years Hugh's senior. Hugh missed them all. Each day he pestered his mother. "Is it time for the bus? Is it time for the bus now?" He always walked the quarter of a mile to the bus stop to meet the four, often arriving early and falling asleep as he waited.

2

In this family, Martha Herr once said of the household she and John Herr had set up, "It was just assumed you were going to do well. The only time something was said was if you did badly." Reflecting on the Mennonite heritage, she said, "You're not supposed to be proud, or show emotion, and you're not used to being praised."

One of the Herrs' goals was to teach their children how to work hard. The young Herrs mowed lawns, hoed fields, and built houses. Even if they came home from school sick, their father would give them tasks. The boys, Hugh included, were the building team. Each day after school, they changed their clothes, ate a snack, and went out to work on a house. They insulated, painted, put up drywall, ran errands, put on roofs, laid shingles, did electrical and plumbing work. When they were little, they stripped wires; when they were older, they put in sockets and helped with the wiring.

John Herr expected excellence on the job. He wanted each task to be done well and did not tolerate sloppiness. The boys were taught to strive to do things right.

John also paid the children for their work, keeping track of their

LANCASTER COUNTY, PENNSYLVANIA   JOHN HERR

hours. In this way the young Herrs earned their own spending money, though they were made to save and bank certain portions.

The Herr building business was part of family life and proceeded on a seasonal cycle. In winter the Herrs would build. In summer they traveled.

When Hugh was six, the family toured parts of Canada and Alaska. From then on, every summer they returned to the mountains to hike, canoe, and fish. Hugh never wanted anything for a present but more gear for hiking, camping, or climbing.

Driving west across the country, the boys would stare at the horizon, hours and hours before the mountains came into view. They would see a cloud in the distance and clamor, "Is that it? Is that it?" The year they went to the Yukon, Hugh sat in the front seat with the travel brochure spread on his lap, craning his neck as he tried to match the views with the pictures.

Once the family reached its campsite, Hugh would often go off by himself and sit and stare at the mountains for hours, thinking unabashedly to himself how much he loved them. He reveled in the lucid skies and cool fresh air; he'd never liked hot weather. His eyes roamed over the ridges and skylines and swatches of trees. The mountains represented challenge, wildness, adventure. Young as he was, he felt their spirituality; it was connected with magic in his mind, and with the things he'd been taught in church. The mountains seemed to be a manifestation of God's raw power and majesty. To walk among them seemed a gift, and to climb to the summits seemed a way to raise himself toward some truth.

As he hiked through the mountains one summer, he pretended he was a hobbit just like the diminutive folk in J.R.R. Tolkien's books. In winter he read more Tolkien and fantasized about his summer adventures.

Each year the family trips focused more and more on mountaineering. Tony was especially keen to climb to the tops of the mountains within range of their campsites, and peak-bagging soon became a goal for all three boys. Their sisters were less interested, and the boys would often have to coax them.

Hugh, being the youngest, was careful never to slow the party down, lest he be left behind the next time. Assuming a mantle of dignity, he strove to stay at the head of the pack.

One year, in the Glacier Peak Wilderness area of the northern Cascades of Washington, the children went off alone overnight. Tony had selected a hike of ten miles, beginning in a flat creekbed. Soon, however, the group reached an area of blow-downs and had to scramble over the fallen trees. Carrying packs containing sleeping bags, food, and other gear, the girls began to drag and asked to stop.

"We can't camp here," Tony said. "There'd be mosquitoes."

"That's right," said Hugh. He knew that Tony wanted to get above treeline before dark so that they could be in position to climb a mountain the next morning.

Soon Ellen asked, "Where's camp?"

"A little farther," Hugh said. But Beth and Ellen said they were tired, and their feet hurt.

"We'll leave you here," Tony threatened. The girls trudged on, miserable. The boys conferred. Hans would stay and hike with the sisters while Tony and Hugh went ahead to look over the terrain.

At length Tony and Hugh reached a long rise, a series of switchbacks up a sixty-degree snow slope. They crossed the slope and found a beautiful spring that looked out over the forest, across the snowcapped Cascades.

By the time they had set up camp, the other three had reached the snow slope. Beth and Ellen were crying, refusing to go any farther.

Hugh explained to them that the route didn't go straight up the incline, that the traverses were easy. He and Tony took their packs and led the way. As dusk settled, Tony and Hugh were making an exploratory foray to the base of the nearest peak.

But the girls were losing interest in the family trips. They missed their friends at home. The next year they made plans to return early, and rode a bus back from Seattle.

The boys, meanwhile, were reading mountaineering books. They drew parallels between themselves and the Lowe brothers, who had done many pioneering winter and ice climbs in the Tetons of Wyoming and the Canadian Rockies. "The Herr brothers," they'd say with mock-solemnity.

10

They no longer considered themselves boys. They were men. They fought to carry the heaviest pack (Hugh fought hardest). Their motto was, "There's no such word as *can't*." John Herr was delighted with their adventuresome natures and their drive.

Father and sons read such books as *Mountaineering: Freedom of the Hills* to learn about mountain safety, weather, and avalanches. They studied and practiced crevasse rescue techniques, using pulleys and prussik knots, and glacier travel. They learned how to belay on a snow slope using an ice axe and a boot. In Glacier National Park, Montana, they rehearsed self-arrest, rolling their weight onto ice axes to stop a downhill slide. Hugh clung to his axe, keeping the point down so that he wouldn't flip, and steered by holding his body in a pike position. He thought he had never had more fun.

Young as he was, Hugh thought these were experiences he would never forget: learning such things as why it was advantageous to travel in the mountains at night, when potential rockfalls were frozen and the snow was hard underfoot. And why a roped party should move in a zigzag line, so that one person falling into a crevasse wouldn't pull the others straight in behind him.

Leaving their packs in camp, the Herr brothers scrambled around on rocks: they knew it was called bouldering and required balance and gymnastic ability.

Back home, Tony, now fourteen, decided to learn the skills of technical rock climbing so that he could climb cliffs. He read *Basic Rockcraft*, by Royal Robbins. He and his brothers found bouldering areas around Lancaster. Hugh always tagged along, innocently assuming that he would be part of the action.

They went to a cluster of rocks called Tailrace, and to the railroad cuts at Safe Harbor, north of their home and by the shores of the Susquehanna River. They looked at diagrams in books and practiced the body maneuvers they read about, moves that came with an exciting new vocabulary.

Laybacking was grabbing a vertical edge, usually a flake of rock, then pulling with hands and pushing with feet, walking the feet up almost alongside the hands. *Bridging* meant stretching feet and legs wide to reach far-apart footholds. *Manteling* meant pushing down on a

LANCASTER COUNTY, PENNSYLVANIA   ANTHONY HERR

ledge until the hands were at waist level, then replacing a hand with a high-stepping foot. The Herrs learned how to climb wide cracks by *jamming*, wedging their fists into them; for two- to three-inch cracks they jammed in their hands at the wrists, and for thinner cracks they twisted and stacked their fingers. They learned how to use *face holds*, the edges and irregularities protruding from a wall or the dishes and pockets sunk into it. They *palmed* their hands on the rock, fingers pointing down or sideways, to push to another handhold, and practiced using *underclings*, down-pointing holds grasped from above. They *smeared* their feet by covering a shallow depression, or even a rough spot on the rock, with as much shoe sole as possible, heels down.

When Tony bought a climbing rope and all three were fitted with harnesses to which it would attach, they studied how to belay, to place protection, and to catch falls. There was *leading*, in which the first climber places various-sized metal wedges called nuts or, often, by the brand name of Stoppers, into cracks, slots, or holes in the rock. To these pieces of protection he would attached snap-links called *carabiners* and nylon slings, and thread his rope through them.

From below a *belayer* would pay the rope out. If the leader fell, he would drop about twice the distance from where he placed his last piece of protection before the rope would catch him. If protection were placed roughly five or ten feet apart, as was customary, he would fall ten or twenty feet, respectively, plus a little, since climbing ropes are made to stretch to ease the jolt.

The leader would go one *pitch*, a distance that could be as long as his 150- to 165-foot rope, before stopping to set up a belay—to place pieces of protection as anchors, tie himself to these, and then bring his partner up from below. In leading, a climber might take substantial falls. But his partner, called the *second*, risked only a short fall, since the rope was snaking up ahead of him.

Alternatively, there was *toproping*, in which a climber walked around to the top of a short cliff and anchored his rope in a kind of pulley system, both rope ends on the ground. He would return to the bottom and begin to climb while his belayer pulled the rope in. Just as if he were seconding, the climber never risked a fall of more than a few feet. Toproping, the Herr brothers learned, was common on short cliffs for convenience, or for routes that lacked satisfactory protection possibilities.

Routes were to be *free-climbed;* that is, climbers would move by using only handholds and footholds, without resorting to pulling on slings or grabbing carabiners, which was considered bad form. In the past, when equipment, techniques, and practices were different, many climbs had been ascended by use of such means; those were called *aid routes.* Aid practices were still used on big walls, such as the three-thousand-foot cliffs of Yosemite, but now, on the shorter cliffs, "nut-craft" and free moves were replacing piton use and sling-assisted moves.

There was the matter of style, too. To *flash* a route meant to climb it on the first try, no falls, and was considered the best style.

The Herrs read further, about the grading system. The 5 grade, followed by a decimal, meant only that the climb was a technical one, not a hike or scramble, and that a rope was needed. Climbs were named and initially rated by the first person to ascend them. Routes from 5.0 to about 5.6 were considered beginner; climbs of 5.10 and up were expert. Grades of 5.10, 5.11, and 5.12 were often followed by a plus or minus that designated gradations of difficulty. Climbs graded 5.12 often required days or even weeks of effort, while top climbers memorized a complicated and strenuous series of moves. Nothing harder than 5.12 had been done.

Tony was by far the most skilled at climbing. In the brothers' bouldering sessions, he dared to go as far as forty feet off the ground on moves as difficult as 5.9. Hugh bouldered with Hans near the bases of the cliffs.

Tony was a star athlete at Penn Manor High School, a thin and long-muscled runner. People loved the way he ran – smooth and flowing, his long blond hair streaming behind.

He projected a combination of innocence and coolness that was part natural, part studied. Everyone liked this soft-spoken, sweet young man, from the jocks to the pot smokers.

As a junior, Tony attended the school district championships with his track teammates. He was anchor for the 440-yard relay, last to run and thus the most important of the four-man team. When the third runner slapped the baton into Tony's hand, a stir went through the crowd.

His tempo was furious. He passed one, two, three other runners. When he pulled almost even with the front runner, the people in the bleachers jumped to their feet, roaring. The two ran head to head, crossing the line with Tony barely behind.

At the finish, he collapsed. Coaches from the other schools surrounded him.

"What a run!"

"Whoa! Fantastic!"

As the circle of men broke and dispersed, Hugh's face appeared. "Good job," was all he said.

At another meet, a Lancaster girl named Sally Hrapchak, who had often been a timer at competitions, congratulated Tony after an event. Hugh was sitting above them in the stands as the two began to talk. He sat, intently interested, his posture discreet. He watched Tony flick his hair sideways out of his face. Hugh flicked his hair off his forehead.

Despite his successes, in track and in his social life, Tony remained preoccupied by climbing. He met a few Pennsylvania climbers and took weekend trips to the steep gold cliffs known as the Shawangunks, in New Paltz, New York. These complex cliffs, laced with roofs, cracks, and corners, are one of the country's best rock-climbing areas. Tony began to take Hans and Hugh with him.

At age eleven, under Tony's tutelage, Hugh began leading climbs at the Shawangunks. Tony wouldn't let him lead often, though. He was concerned that Hugh was too young to be making crucial decisions on safety matters.

Yet Hugh was nimble and strong. The first time he had tried pull-ups, during the fourth grade, he had performed fifteen consecutively. He was the first fourth-grader in his school ever to win the President's Physical Fitness Award. In the Shawangunks, his main objective was to keep up with Tony. From this time on, most of Hugh's friends were older than he; most were Tony's friends.

In the spring of his senior year in high school, Tony didn't join the track team because of climbing. His coach couldn't believe it.

Looking ahead to summer, Tony began planning a three-month

climbing trip across the United States. He and his friends would leave right after graduation and climb mounts Whitney, Hood, and Rainier.

Tony started laying out his gear, selecting clothes, and buying freeze-dried food. On the floor of his room he arranged carabiners, nuts, tubular ice screws, a dead-man snow anchor, an ice axe and ice hammer, crampons, a shovel, his headlamp. Hugh sat on the bed and watched, and wished he were going.

3

Near the Uberfall, a spring in the Shawangunks cliffs, is a 5.10 route known as *Retribution.* Tony led the way, clamping onto the meager layback edge in the overhanging corner, thrilled to be doing such a high-grade route. Though the brothers had read about the rating system and understood it intellectually, they were unsure how high on the scale they could climb.

Above, Tony set up his anchors, clipped his rope into them, and began to belay one of his companions. From where he stood, taking rope in, braced for a sudden pull should a climber fall, he could not see over the edge; his companions were hidden in the overhanging corner that was the crux.

One after another, the other climbers tried the route, sometimes several times each. All of them lowered off from the crux. Then, as Tony reeled in more and more rope, he could tell that someone had made it.

"All *right*," he thought. He leaned out, trying to see who it was. The top of a familiar dark head came into view.

"It's Huey!"

From that day, Hugh's climbing accelerated. People watching him would muse about the future of this twelve-year-old kid, and about how good he might become. Tony was now breaking into 5.10, leading such classics of the grade as *Country Roads* and *Erect Direction*. Hugh was right behind him.

The brothers were going to the Shawangunks every weekend and bouldering many afternoons, even at night by the light of a Coleman lantern. On the rock, Tony had the most raw talent, the most natural technique and balance. Hans had the strongest fingers of the three, which sometimes got him up moves on small holds and overhanging rock that his brothers couldn't pull. Hugh, though youngest, had the best endurance. His build was muscular, his shoulders slightly rounded. He had shaggy brown hair, a smooth, inscrutable face, and green eyes.

As the Herr brothers became accustomed to the rating system, they realized that they had been climbing hard for years. Rich Romano, a regular at the Gunks, climbed with them one day on a seventy-foot graffiti-marked wall called Tailrace Spire, at Tailrace near the banks of the Susquehanna. Tony had done the first ascent of the route over a year before. Hugh now led the route, wearing a brand of street footwear called Earth Shoes, then lowered so that Rich could lead it, too. Rich, properly shod in tight, rubber-soled EB climbing shoes, had trouble and moved up and down repeatedly on the sparsely protected, dangerous route, looking for the right combination of moves.

"I'm getting my face punched out!" he moaned. "Beyond recognition." Usually exact in his footwork, he finally scuffled his way up and declared the route a 5.11. Yet it wasn't nearly so hard as many of the bouldering moves the brothers had been doing.

At thirteen Hugh was racing through the climbing grades, a progression that culminated when he flashed the 5.11-plus *Persistent* at the Shawangunks, reaching the top on his first try. As Hugh lowered to the ground, a tall, cheerful climber approached.

"I've seen you around," he said. "My name's Russ Clune. I just want to tell you that I am really impressed with your climbing."

Hugh began climbing with Russ and another proficient climber, Morris Hershoff, as well as with his brothers.

At fourteen Hugh climbed the spectacular eight-foot overhang *Foops*, a world-famous Gunks testpiece, known as a stiff 5.11. By now he was training hard, bouldering almost daily and building endurance by going for long runs around his family's fields. Thoughts of weekend climbs – past and future – distracted him on weekdays.

For Hugh, climbing became a fierce obsession that awakened in him a drive he hadn't known he possessed. On the rock he became competitive: he enjoyed climbing for its own sake, but he wanted to succeed, too. Failure brought not temper tantrums but a resolve to work harder.

His father sometimes teased him about the bouldering moves, known among rock climbers as problems, on which he spent so much time. "Done any good *problems* lately?" he would drawl.

Hugh didn't appreciate such mockery of the pure and admirable activity of climbing. "He has no respect," he said, stung, to his brothers.

What Hugh found in climbing was exhilaration. There was a profound joy in focusing his mind into the rock, into the power of his hands, staying calm, calculating . . . and then *going*.

A good climber synthesizes many variables in developing his craft. Endurance and explosive strength are a foundation, but equally important are flexibility and grace. The endless variety of factors that form rock-climbing technique include a knowledge of how to shift balance, lever, and twist to reach higher; to pull inward with feet or push down on them, cross one foot over the other like a ballet dancer, or even hook them overhead to pull the body up. A rock climber learns to read the rock, to know intuitively what to do with what kinds of holds: when to palm, push, pull, or stretch; when to lunge to grab a protruding pebble overhead, or slap one's hand around a corner.

Each climb is a new experience, in which the climber must make decisions on the spot as he ascends. At places he must be cool and logical, or in searching out ways to weight feet and rest arms, even devious. Other times he must make a plan for movement, and then execute it fast to avoid burning up his strength. Four climbers might cover the same section of wall in four different ways: one might look burly and aggressive, one light and feathery, one jittery; one might try a sequence of motions that doesn't work, tire, and drop.

Hugh was tantalized by concepts of the mental control needed to perform in a risk-taking, problem-solving situation. He decided he would never rate himself good, would never feel he had mastered the mental aspect of climbing.

The risks inherent in rock climbing stimulated him, and that was an

RINGROSE PEAK, CANADIAN ROCKIES   ANTHONY HERR

admission many climbers refuse to make. By placing himself in extreme situations, he forced his best efforts. Swinging out over one of the many overhangs at the Shawangunks, he would look down and exult, "This has just *gotta* be dangerous."

The height and danger added to the mystery and thus the power of the sport. But a climber learns to focus on moves, rather than the potential of a fall; he learns, too, over time, to place his protection well and to trust it. When he finishes a climb, when he's made the right decisions or chosen the right technique, or pushed through despite fears, he feels a rush of satisfaction and jubilation.

By comparison, school was dull. Hugh was competitive about his grades and did well, but he simply wasn't interested. He joined the gymnastics team, primarily to improve his climbing skills, and excelled on the rings and parallel bars. The season for gymnastics complemented climbing perfectly: practices and meets were scheduled in winter, when he couldn't rock-climb anyway.

Hans was a teammate. Once, during unseasonable weather, the two told their coach that they had missed a Saturday practice because they had had to chop wood. Their coach shook his head skeptically. "Those Herr boys," he said.

Dating was equally cyclical. Hugh had girlfriends only in winter, when weekend dates wouldn't interfere with climbing. Although the girls found him endearing and congenial, his relationships with them didn't last long; two months was the longest he ever had a girlfriend in high school.

Hugh sometimes thought of his classmates' lives and wondered whether he might be missing something. But he didn't care.

———— • ————

Hugh slipped out of his sleeping bag and crept through the rows of unshaven climbers on the second floor of the Conrad Kain Hut. Their snores made him think of frogs in the ponds at home. The hut, a few hours' hike up a trail, was set among the string of granite needles and jumble of buttresses that are the Purcell Range in the Bugaboo Group of western Canada.

By eight he was hiking, alone. His shoes squeaked across the wide glacier above the hut, toward the sharp peaks that jutted up at its edge. To his left were Snowpatch Spire, named for the bright sloping field of snow that never melts off its top, and the smaller Pigeon Spire.

Hugh headed to his right, past the curving snow col that separated Snowpatch from the rubbly left ridge of the 10,420-foot Bugaboo Spire. He could see the faint bluish line of the bergschrund, the gap between the bottom of the col wall and the flat glacier. It had widened a bit during these late summer days. When he'd first arrived, a week ago, he had just stepped over it. But by this time the same crossing took a long, deliberate stride, and a person coming down from the slope above had to be careful not to slip.

Now he was heading toward the grand convex sweep of Bugaboo's northeast ridge. On the nearer southeast face of the pyramid he could see brown-splotched snow spots and long black cracks.

As he reached the boulders and scraps of talus at Bugaboo's face, he was thinking of Don Juan the Sorceror, a character in the Carlos Castenada books. Magic and spirits and ethereal connections—things that humans couldn't comprehend—were in the world, in the air. He thought of how Don Juan had said that a person who looks over his shoulder and sees a shadow is seeing his own death.

Hugh now darted a glance over his shoulder. He was looking for his shadow, a black crow overhead, any sort of omen. Turning, he thought he saw something, a fleeting grayness.

He hesitated, a weird hollowness opening within his rib cage, then wheeled and retreated. He walked very fast, and slowed only as he neared the hut. By now the other climbers had awakened, and some were bouldering on the rocks near the hut's back door. A few problems were high enough off the ground that people were using topropes.

"Hey!" Hugh called to one of them. "Would you belay me on this?" Within minutes he had toproped a 5.12 section that he had failed on the day before. He stayed at the hut until early afternoon, then set off again, saying nothing of his plans.

The weather was perfect, the skies brilliant blue. As he listened again to the sounds of his feet crunching across the grainy snow and stepped among the yellow and brown dapples of the sun cups that dotted it, he prepared. He sought to make himself very humble, very small. He believed that a person had to do that before attempting a solo.

He would be climbing alone, with neither rope nor hardware. He would be exposing himself to the highest danger on a ridge so airy and exposed that fifteen hundred feet of space would drop open beneath his feet. He would have to reach deep into himself.

At the bottom of the route he exchanged his sneakers for his tight climbing shoes and pulled the laces through each eyelet with exaggerated deliberateness. In his pack were water, some granola, a windbreaker, a wool hat, and a bivouac sack – a light envelope in which a person could survive outside overnight. There had been a storm only last night, washing the air impossibly clean, and now, as he looked up toward the first long rock flake on his first big solo climb, the mountain world appeared fresh and full of verges and potentials. He was fifteen years old.

———— • ————

Eight hundred feet above the glacier, in an ever-widening realm, Hugh balanced his foot on one knob of coarse granite and reached for another. He was electrified by the downward sweep of the ridge that dropped away, clumps of snow stuck to its sides, on his left, and at some distant level he was thrilled with a mixture of glory and terror.

"You really could die," he thought. Then he admonished himself in silent oratorical tones: "Use that to be safer, to commit to each move with total concentration."

The climb, a 5.7, was a number of grades below Hugh's level of skill, but in his solo endeavor the consequences of a single slip or sudden loss of balance would be death. Forcing himself to calculate each move precisely and to shift his balance flawlessly, he banished the fear, pushed it to the back of his mind. He did not sweat or shake as he rocked his weight upward onto a shallow half-dish in the rock wall. Above, he was confronted by a gully stuffed with pockets of snow and slush. Legs splayed, keeping his feet on the dry rock on either side of the wet runnels, he bridged his way up.

At the summit ridge he threaded his way across, tiptoeing between boulders and among chaotic piles of rocks. Taking a quick look eastward, he could just discern the dark forms of the Rockies, fifty miles away. Without pausing he hustled down the slope of the other side of the rock ridge.

Only when Hugh reached the col between Bugaboo and Snowpatch did he pronounce himself safe and allow the relief to stream through him. Only as he continued across the glacier in the blue evening did the knot of tension within him dissipate. He stopped and turned around. Alpenglow filled the basin, lit up the peaks and spires in ruddy planes and streaks, flowed into the hollows.

"I just did four thousand feet of climbing in two and a half hours," he thought, battering against his own disbelief. He had read in *Fifty Classic Climbs* that four to six hours was the normal ascent time. Power settled into him, raw and intoxicating. He had gotten away with something gigantic, cocky, wonderful.

———•———

Hugh's successful solo was just the start. He and Hans – Tony was in Alaska, climbing Mount McKinley – made the second free ascent of the *East Face* of Bugaboo Spire (5.10), did the *Beckey-Greenwood* route on Snowpatch and made several repeats of routes and first ascents on Crescent Spire. Hugh and Don Peterson, a veteran Yosemite climber, attempted to free-climb the *Southeast Buttress* of Pigeon Spire; they ascended the difficult 5.12 pitch high on the wall but were forced back down by heavy snow.

Returning to Pigeon Spire in better weather, Hugh and Don took on an overhanging crack. It was fingertip-thin, bulging, immaculate. Don led the route. Hugh, yarding up on one fingerlock after another, was nearly to the top when he thought for one teetering, straining moment that he would not make it. But with a final crank, he was up, filled with joy and relief.

"Don, I love you!" he gasped in his jubilation. A wave of embarrassment passed over him as he realized what he had just said.

His partner chuckled. "How hard do you think it was?" he asked as Hugh, crimson-faced, turned away to loosen his shoes.

"Five-eleven?"

"Yeah, that's about right."

Four years later Bugaboo climbers telling tales around the table in the Conrad Kain Hut would still, in tones of incredulity and amusement, speak of "the kids" from Pennsylvania. Five years later the route would be rerated 5.12. The climbing standard in the Bugaboos had been pushed two grades higher by a fifteen-year-old.

"So that was the Bugaboos' first five-twelve?" a friend asked Hugh.

"It was its first five-eleven," he replied.

———— • ————

Hans discovered hang gliding. He went on his own, as his brothers weren't interested. He loved it. He didn't mind the sensation of air beneath him. What had bothered him in climbing was the dread that he might fall against an obstacle, a wall. When he had wings on, he felt no fear, only thrills, even at the edge of a cliff.

Tony, at twenty-one, married Sally Hrapchak.

With Tony often gone and Hans otherwise occupied, Hugh climbed with anybody he could find. Too young for a driver's license, he was dependent on rides from others. Sometimes his attempts to arrange transportation were futile, and his father would drive him the five hours to the Shawangunks and back, and belay him on the cliffs. It wasn't unusual, during the drives, for Hugh to say nothing at all. He had become very intense. He was always thinking, always practicing concentration.

Still fifteen, Hugh climbed *Kansas City*, taking only five falls in the process of figuring his way up the twenty-foot overhang. As soon as he got home that October weekend he called Tony.

"Tony. What's happening," said Hugh in the uninflected, terse language the brothers used among themselves.

"How was it?"

"Great."

"What'd you do?"

"*Kansas City.*"

There was a tiny pause. *Kansas City*, a famous 5.12. Tony wished he'd been there. He could see the long, long line of that overhang and picture his brother hanging possumlike underneath it, swooping from one hold to the next. Tony wondered whether he himself could have done that – Hugh was getting so much stronger – and whether he could ever catch up.

"All right!" Tony said. "Great, man. What else'd you do?"

"*Red Tape* and *Sling Time*," said Hugh.

"Well, cool. Let's get together. Maybe I can come up next weekend."

But it wasn't until a cold November weekend, a month later, that Tony went to the Gunks with Hugh. By this time Hugh had climbed *Kansas City* twice and knew the moves by rote; he had the sequence wired. Though the temperature was thirty-five degrees, he climbed barefoot so that he could curl his toes like a monkey over the holds. Tony belayed, shivering, barely able to keep his hands out of his pockets to mind the rope.

No one else was climbing. At the base of the cliff two clusters of people gathered to watch. They were silent as Hugh crept along the underside of the roof, his feet higher than his head, swinging his body forward in a line parallel to the roof, placing his feet on the same holds as his hands.

"Holy shit!" said one of the spectators. "Who is that?"

"Hugh Herr," Tony said. Behind him he could hear the sharp intakes of breath, and off to the side he could see reverent eye blinking and head shaking.

As Hugh turned the lip of the roof, someone said, "That's the most incredible thing I've ever seen."

"He's really good in the cold," Tony said. "He's so fired up, he doesn't feel it."

Down by the little knots of people, all hunched against the cold, swinging their arms and stamping their feet, a single climber approached and looked up, his eye following the rope to where Hugh stood, adjusting carabiners to lower off. It was Russ Clune.

"Huey Herr, what are you doing up there?" he shouted. "You're crazy!"

4

Super Crack looks almost innocent when you approach it from the trail. The crack splits a buttress squarely and arrows up for eighty feet, edged with streaks that are silvery and cobwebby white. The crack's sides are also often dusted with white powder, gymnast's chalk, the handprints left by climbers working to get a purchase.

If you are a good technical rock climber, this crack is alluring, enticing. It looks as though your fingers will fit nicely into it, and you will swing your feet up and slip the tips of your toes in it, and reach, and bring your feet up again in exuberant swings; and before long you will have climbed *Super Crack*.

Now, from the arresting black line of the crack, let your eyes sweep appreciatively over the buttress around it. See the gray and gold and brown streaks, the horizontal ripples, the sharp flake edges, the striations and the cobbly patches.

Walk closer and scramble up on the jumbled boulders. Now you see the angle of this wall. It is relentlessly, hilariously overhung. About ten feet up, the wall alongside the crack kicks out—not in an overhang as such, but in a little overlap, six inches or so. About ten feet farther, though, is a real overhang, a true, honest roof that shoots out nearly two feet. You can see a good handhold—a bucket—above the jutting roof, but it's a long reach away, maybe two and a half feet.

Finally, go stand beneath the crack and you will see that it is inch-and-a-quarter size. Climbers know what that means. It's too narrow to jam your hands into, and too wide for jamming your fingers. Even if you are a very good technical rock climber, you might be sort of stuck.

———————— • ————————

In the summer of 1972, Steve Wunsch, considered a phenomenon in the climbing world, decided to climb *Super Crack*. Since graduating from Princeton three years before, Steve had become a full-time traveling climber. During the period over which he worked on *Super Crack*, he also made many extreme first ascents in Colorado, New York, and the United Kingdom.

Day after day, his climbing partner Kevin Bein stood at the base of the route, holding Steve's rope as he climbed and fell and rested again before making yet another try. On a route as difficult as *Super Crack*, that is what you need to do: memorize precise sequences of gymnastic moves, build on knowledge, get up each section with increasing efficiency, link the sections, and go on. You do not necessarily get higher each time. But eventually you pull it off—or accept defeat.

It took Steve eight days and some thirty-five falls over a two-year period before he succeeded in 1974. Kevin had taken to calling the route *Wunsch upon a Climb.*

The climb was years ahead of its time, more difficult than the routes being done in the United States, in Britain, in Europe. It was so much harder than other routes in the nation that it was at first graded an astonishing 5.13, when hitherto the grading scale for rock climbs had ranged from 5.0 to a very few 5.12s. Today the route is considered a 5.12-plus rather than a full 5.13. But even now, with higher standards in rock climbing and improved training and equipment, a *Super Crack* ascent is prized.

In 1977, three years after Wunsch's achievement, Yosemite's Ron Kauk, who was in the vanguard of American free climbing, came east and made the much-awaited second ascent of *Super Crack*. He managed the climb after four days.

28

In 1978 the best American duo in climbing, Max Jones and Mark Hudon, arrived in New York. "We had to check out *Super Crack*, the world's hardest rock climb (or so every Gunkie told us)," wrote Jones. "It had been climbed only twice in four years, and that wasn't due to lack of trying.

"Upon first inspection, it doesn't look too hard," Jones continued. "I remember telling Mark that we might get it that day. Don't be fooled! After five attempts to complete the first 15 feet I take another look at this thing. It's hard! It's a real bad size and it's very hard to find jams that work. Every time, I try something new." Jones completed the ascent on the third day; Hudon succeeded sometime later.

In 1981 Australia's best climber, Kim Carrigan, arrived in the Shawangunks and headed for *Super Crack*. His was the first one-day ascent, and it made big news among climbers.

In 1982 sixteen-year-old Hugh Herr was sharpening his mind and building his strength in preparation for a day at the Shawangunks. He had his eye on *Super Crack*.

———— • ————

Hugh pushed open the sliding door and stepped out onto the porch. He passed through the doorway, framed by a trellis on which clematis would soon climb and wind. Beside him, neatly squared green yews lined the base of the brick house.

Hugh ran diagonally across the lawn toward two of the Herrs' three white barns, passing an empty dark garden plot.

Around him, everything was in motion. The wind made a soft lisping sound, low in his ears, rising and ebbing. It ruffled the blue spruce, hemlock, and white pine ringing the house. It sounded different in the different trees he passed: high and tinkly in the thin new leaves of the locust, and low in the budding red maple. A clothesline stretched between the two trees, and a rope swing hung from the locust.

Coming to the edge of the yard, he veered right out onto a farm lane, a low strip of green stretching across the fields. He heard his footsteps, his breath, the sound of a tractor in the distance, the bark of a dog.

To the far right, beyond the cluster of the farmhouse and outbuildings, the curving lines of terraced fields dipped down; this year they

SHAWANGUNKS, NEW YORK   ANTHONY HERR

would be used for alfalfa. Beyond them was the humped line of the road, and across that another farmstead. A horse and buggy rolled along the road, the red reflector lights installed on the buggy blinking in the failing late-afternoon light.

To his left was forest, but when Hugh looked to the front, he might as well have been going out to sea. The fields rose upward slightly, hiding any sights beyond the skyline, so that his path seemed endless.

The only indication of depth came from a silhouette on the skyline. It was of the weeds lining the farm lane. When he focused on the straggly shapes, they looked surprisingly large, spoiling the illusion of a far horizon. The lane turned slightly right. He could see ridges of trees and hills miles away. The woods were green with black shadows in the foreground, and blue-gray in the distance.

A few more minutes, and he made a quarter-turn left, to a perpendicular farm lane. He was passing more houses on his right, and empty cornfields on the left. Ragged husks lay on the ground among round gray and pink stones.

He turned sharp left again, now taking a line roughly parallel to the first; one more turn and he would finish the square. He was on the high leg of the run, heading toward the forest, the wind on his left cheek almost numbing the bone below his temple, coming from the direction of home. He went left once more when he reached the woods. As he skirted loopy limbs reaching out from the trees, his shins were slapped by a stinging nettle.

It was almost dark now. The lane curved left at the end, and the wind now focused on his right cheek as he made a final sprint toward the lights of the house.

He was thinking about the moves on *Super Crack*, about how he would get to the bucket hold high above the roof. He was sure that he would grab the undercling below the roof with his right hand, and cross over with his left to go for the bucket.

————— • —————

It was the first climbing weekend of the year. Hugh, wearing a patterned wool hat and wrapped in a sleeping bag, woke up early. His campsite, a floor of muddy washes pocketed among a stretch of trees, was just across the road from the string of Shawangunks cliffs.

31

As soon as Hugh opened his eyes, he knew. "This is the day," he said to himself. He sat straight up and unfolded the fuzzy gray pile jacket that had been his pillow, and put it on. Then he pulled on purple sweat pants with red stripes up the sides, white socks, and tennis shoes. He stood and looked at the trees, barely budding in the light pea green of earliest spring. His heart started pounding in weird thuds.

In the car now with his friend and gymnastics coach, Tim Garland, Hugh thought about the moves on *Super Crack*. Going up Main Street, they passed a bent, dark-skinned man with elbow-length hair tied back in a ponytail. He wore a silver bolo tie and belt buckle, and silver decorated the band of his cowboy hat. He was stiffly and fixedly sweeping the sidewalk. Climbers called him Chief Broom. As the car passed, Hugh observed the man's total concentration.

At the Plaza Diner, Hugh greeted Charlotte, everybody's favorite waitress. She always kept the coffee cups full. Although Hugh did not drink coffee, his climbing friends did; they called it plasma, and the coffee shop, the Plasma Diner.

Hugh and Tim seated themselves in a booth, and Hugh flipped idly through the table's little stainless-steel jukebox. He felt on edge, a sharp edge, as if he were about to take a crucial and difficult exam, and was thinking about the information he would need. He wasn't worried about his strength on the overhanging route. He knew how strong he was. What he worried about was his mind.

The route was all psyche, he believed. Six months earlier, he had come to the conclusion that he was physically able to do any route yet climbed, anywhere. "If I have the intelligence, if I have the mind," he reasoned to himself, "I can flash any route at the top grades. No falls."

He had dreamed of this climb, this ascent of *Super Crack*. But his preparation was not the intangible stuff of dreams; he had viewed the climb as a problem: figured the constants, known the variables, decided how to increase his chances on what he wasn't able to calculate.

It wasn't difficult for him to take care of the technical aspects. He had scrutinized the route from the boulders below it, eyed its slots and tapers, and chosen his array of protection carefully and sparingly, to eliminate every bit of extra weight from his rack.

He also calculated his runouts, the amount of ground covered between protection placements. To minimize the amount of strength-sapping time he would spend while clinging to the rock to place his protection, Hugh planned his runouts differently. They would be long.

Already he had bouldered up the start of the route. Practicing extremely difficult moves, in which he had to stack fingers and thumbs against each other to wedge them, he had reached a height of fifteen feet, just below the roof. He had visualized the moves above, imagining how to do them. He memorized all the sequences he envisioned.

At home, Hugh had built an inch-and-a-quarter crack between long boards he set up in a corncrib. Lately he had been climbing the twenty-foot crack ten times an hour, several times a day.

He had decided that once he had set up all the factors he could control and had trained adequately, there would be no reason to think. Having laid his groundwork, he should clear his mind – just shut it down and simply go. So at home in Pennsylvania, he had practiced meditating, staving off all thought processes. For one minute he would try to think of nothing. Or he would concentrate on only one thing, say, the feeling on his tongue.

This way, he thought, he could send the negatives – fear of failure, and such judgmental thoughts as "this climb is easy" or "this climb is hard" – into abeyance. Then he could concentrate on doing just one move at a time. And when he finished meditating before the climb, he would explode. He would be like a cat in a frenzy, a springing cat. Nothing would stop him, and there would be no thought.

Now, at the diner, he ate a breakfast of oatmeal, as intended. He liked oatmeal, often even ate raw oats with milk; good clean fuel. The previous day he had selected a diet of carbohydrates, bananas, and vitamin E.

As he and Tim drove the fifteen minutes back to the rock, and then walked the three miles past various cliffs toward the area known as Skytop, his nervous tension didn't increase. There was so much energy coursing through him that he felt he couldn't fail.

It was a muted, foggy day. A few scraps of snow lay among the trees, and their branches were faintly damp from a brief shower in the night, which had left the air smelling of wet wood and rotting leaves. But the sky was brightening. And *Super Crack* overhung so much, it didn't really get wet anyway.

At the base of the route Hugh clipped his chosen rack onto a nylon sling and slipped that diagonally over one shoulder and across his chest. Each piece was in order, according to when he would use it. The rack totaled only six pieces. Most climbers started up *Super Crack* carrying at least twice that many.

Before he tied into his rope, he bouldered up fifteen feet and slotted in one piece of protection, the only one he would use before reaching the roof. It was a small hexagonal piece that he jiggled in sideways as he hung from the stacked fingers of one hand.

He climbed back down, then sat and massaged his forearms, which were aching, swollen with blood from the strain. And then he just sat still. Tim waited quietly.

When Hugh started, everything went as planned. He climbed past the first piece, thumb and fingers methodically inserting and pulling out, then plugging in again higher. His lower lip was sucked under and the skin between his upper lip and nostrils puckered out.

Hanging on jams right below the overhang, he placed his second piece of protection. Other climbers would have already used three.

He gripped the undercling in his right hand, and with a power swoop of the left over the roof, caught the high big hold. Hanging one-handed, his feet merely pressed against small, sloping holds on the wall below, he tried to fiddle in a big hex, but it wouldn't fit the constrictions of the crack. A full minute passed. He decided to quit trying to place the nut lest he lose power. He knew there was a potential rest, the next bucket hold, where the crack jogged right ten feet above him.

He made a decision to switch plans. He yanked up with his left arm and got a higher grip with his right. He heard Tim say, "Uh-ooooh."

But Hugh had calculated the odds. He was sure he was in enough control to make it to the rest. The nut was at his feet: he would be protected from a ground fall until he had almost reached the bucket.

He leaned his body left, pulling sideways against the crack. He swung a foot onto the big jug, then stood up on it and fished his fingers higher in the crack.

"Don't be sloppy," Hugh told himself. "Set every fingerlock per-fectly." Were he to fall now, he would come very close to the ground. "Stay calm," he told himself. "You can do these moves."

He reached the high bucket, placed his right hand on its left side, and crossed his left wrist over that to press his palm against the horizontal bottom of the pod, covering as much surface as possible. His mind was in such an elevated state, he was not particularly afraid.

Then he toiled and toiled, working a piece of protection into the crack above him. But that took yet more strength, and he had already lost some below.

Finally the piece was set. He crimped his fingers into the sharp-edged crack above, skin grinding against the rough edges, and cranked up into it. Now his arms were pumping out, engorged with blood and searing lactic acid; his hands stiffened into chicken claws. They wouldn't hold on any longer.

He fell, arcing down and outward until the rope caught him, ten feet below. "Awww!" he yelled. Tim lowered him on his rope to the boulders.

The two stared at each other. They were hardly disappointed; they were elated that he had gotten so high, past all the hardest moves but one. "I'm going to do this," said Hugh. He drank some water, then sat down while Tim walked off to refill the plastic bottle.

Hugh looked at the trees around him, with their skinny twisting trunks. He turned and knelt, rested his chest against his folded legs, and touched his forehead to the rough surface of the boulder. He stretched his arms behind him, palms up. When Tim returned with the water an hour later, he had not moved.

———— • ————

Now ten minutes later, standing at the base of the route, he felt dazed. He could not remember the climb, but the hollow feeling in his arms and the sight of the rope, trailing from Tim's belay spot to the top of the cliff, offered proof of his achievement. "Do you realize what I just did?" he asked.

Tim shook his head in wonder, then walked the long way around to the top and rappelled down, retrieving Hugh's gear as he lowered.

At the Uberfall, whose spring is a natural meeting place for climbers, Tim announced that Hugh had nearly flashed *Super Crack*, had done it with only one fall. As word spread among the milling climbers there, and continued that Saturday night through restaurants and bars—the Gay 90s, the Bacchus, the Northern Lights—many people didn't believe it. But some had seen Hugh climb and knew he had the skill. Rich Romano was among them, yet even he was momentarily speechless. He finally spoke: "I doubt anybody will ever do that again."

When he heard the news by telephone Sunday night, Tony felt a familiar pang along with his pride.

At school Monday morning one of Hugh's friends made the usual joke: "Huey! Climbed a mountain lately?" His classmates had no idea of the scope of Hugh's feats in the climbing world, or even exactly what rock climbing was. Hugh didn't mind; he found it amusing that everyone thought he spent his weekends walking up grassy hills.

But there were other people whose opinions mattered to him. Henry Barber, of New Hampshire, had been the hottest, most technically talented climber of the late 1970s, and a visionary: he was one of the first climbers to show the courage and conviction to climb difficult routes ropeless, and among the first to travel overseas to attempt foreign climbs. In so doing, Henry Barber had raised standards in other countries by as much as two grades. Henry preached clean, ethical climbing—leaving the cliff with no marks, as if no one had ever been there—and pure style. The ultimate expression of this style was to climb solo, independent of rope, belayer, even technology. He was Hugh's idol.

"Hats off to him," Henry Barber said.

5

The year he was sixteen, Hugh became fascinated with the art of soloing, the ultimate expression of mind control in climbing. The solo climber ascends without any rope to catch him if he falls. Because it demands perfection of its practitioners, soloing seemed to him infinitely rewarding. After he returned from Canada and his solo of Bugaboo, he began climbing ropeless in the Shawangunks. Although he chose routes just a pitch off the ground, some were rated as difficult as 5.10 and 5.11.

"I want to solo *Super Crack*," he told Tony one day. As their relationship stood, one of them had always exulted when the other did something considered radical. Hugh expected Tony to reinforce this aspiration, to say, "Oh, cool!"

"Oh," Tony said. "Really?"

Once, when Tony was able to join him for a climbing weekend, the two approached a seam of a crack—a 5.11 named *P.R.* Tony led the route well, but Hugh fell, over and over and over, before he finally got up. He was furious, his ego shattered. The next weekend he returned to the Gunks and soloed the route.

When he got back to Lancaster on Sunday night, he called Tony. "I soloed *P.R.*," he said.

Over the hill from the Herr farmhouse lived an Amish family. The two Amish girls, Sarah and Anna, wore long purple or green dresses, white bonnets with straps that tied under their chins, and no shoes. Hugh, age four, was afraid of them.

To tease him, one day they chased him to the top of a hill.

"Get away!" he screamed. "Get away from me!"

He told his older brothers what had happened. Tony and Hans looked at each other sternly. "We'll take care of it," Tony said.

The next time he saw the Amish girls, Tony drew himself up to his full ten-year-old height. "You leave my brother alone," he said. And they did.

"You *what*? You *asshole!*" Hugh said nothing. "Hugh, I don't think that's very calculated. You fell on it about fifteen times."

"It's not that high off the ground. And the landing's not that bad."

"You're kidding," said Tony, incredulous. Hugh changed the subject. Three choppy sentences later, they hung up.

Tony had had his own bouts and battles over soloing. A few years before, he had blithely come home and talked about some solos that he had done. His father was incensed.

"Dad," Tony had tried to explain, "a climber is *so* solid when he's climbing a lot below his ability. A five-ten climber isn't going to fall off a five-six."

"All that has to happen is for one foot to slip, Tony," John Herr said. "That's all it would take." And Tony had drifted away from ropeless climbing.

Now Tony thought and thought, going back and forth as to what he should do. He'd thought nothing of it when Hugh soloed the 5.10 *Retribution*. That climb was easy for Hugh. But now his little brother, the kid he had taught to climb, was pushing it too far and could get killed. He felt that Hugh was too young to contemplate the consequences of an accident. "He's overdosing on confidence, on power," Tony thought. "He thinks he's immortal. He doesn't get the idea of life in a wheelchair."

But even as he told himself how foolhardy it was for anyone to solo a route he had flailed on only a week before, Tony also knew that feelings of frustration and jealousy were behind his outburst during the telephone conversation with his brother. Anger and concern fused in his mind and melded into a decision. He had to let his parents know that he could no longer control his brother. He wanted them to understand that.

His mother answered the phone.

"I'm starting to worry about Hugh," said Tony. "He's starting to climb at the edge of his ability, going without a rope. I think it's getting out of hand."

Martha Herr sighed. "What do you expect us to do?" she asked. "Tell him to stop climbing?"

Immediately, Tony regretted having spoken. He felt foolish. She was right: what could parents do? "I don't know," he said. "I just thought I'd let you know. I want you to know that I'm not encouraging it at this point. If something happens, I don't want you to think that I was responsible."

Still, when he hung up he felt relieved. "I've washed my hands of it now," he told himself. But he also felt guilty and sorrowful.

Hugh's parents discussed the problem. They had pointed out the danger many times, but it had done no good. They could not keep Hugh from climbing; it was his life. Perhaps the best solution was to impose a moratorium on soloing. Later, with a few years' maturity, he might see the dangers and have more respect for the value of his own life.

That night, John Herr walked into Hugh's room, where his son lay reading in bed. "Hugh, I hear you've been free climbing," he said. Though he used the wrong term—soloing was what he meant—Hugh knew exactly what he was talking about. He just looked up, saying nothing. "As long as you are a part of this house," his father said, "you may not solo."

After that, Hugh climbed ropeless far less. Once, after soloing a climb, he told a friend, "Don't tell Tony."

That year he took up rope soloing. It was not, however, for safety's sake. Hugh simply couldn't always find climbing partners skilled enough for the hard routes he wanted to do—the ones he needed a rope for. In rope soloing the climber fixes his rope to a point on the ground, then adjusts a sliding prussik knot as he climbs. He must stop in the middle of difficult moves not just to place his protection, as usual, but to slide the knot along.

Rope soloing is a complicated and awkward process that actually increases the difficulty of a climb, but at least if the climber falls, his rope will catch him.

On a trip to Yosemite Valley, a climbers' mecca in California, Hugh climbed the 5.12 *Kansas City*-sized roof *Separate Reality* this way. Twice he reached the lip of the roof, and twice he had caught the finishing bucket hold when his knot pulled him off backward. He had to give himself more slack, risking a longer fall, so that he could finish the climb.

Hugh had come to Yosemite with Hans, who wanted to go swimming and meet girls as well as climb. Hugh was single-minded, though.

On a rest day, as they sat at the beach, Hans looked over to see his brother clawing the sand.

"What's wrong with *you*?" he said.

The next day Hugh and Hans set off on *Astroman*, one of the United States' testpieces, and renowned among climbers in other countries as well. The route involves five pitches of 5.11 and six of 5.10, all steep and strenuous.

Hugh led. He wormed into one of the route's most notorious spots, the Harding slot, an awkward, overhanging, wide crack. Once through the Harding slot, the climber must continue up or climb down. He cannot rappel because the route overhangs so much that he and his ropes would only end up dangling in space.

He was just through it when Hans said, "Hugh. I want to go down."

"What?"

"I want to go down. This isn't fun."

There was no more discussion, nor did Hugh consider arguing. The two immediately turned around.

Hans liked climbing, but he had never been into climbing for its own sake as much as for simply being one of the brothers, and this route was more than he was willing to do. Hugh accepted it.

Hugh, though widely known on the East Coast, was not a familiar name or face to the climbers in the valley. One day, walking out of the gift shop in Yosemite, he came face to face with a certain California climber. Hugh's hands were wrapped in adhesive tape to protect them from abrasion in the jam cracks for which the valley is renowned. Said the Californian, "Only pussies tape their hands."

But Hans and Hugh were befriended by an experienced valley regular, Steve Grossman, from Arizona. Knowing he would get along well with Hugh, Tony had called Steve beforehand to say, "My brothers are coming through–take care of them, O.K.?"

Steve met the two in Camp 4 and offered to climb the northwest face of the two-thousand-foot granite monolith Half Dome with them. It would take them a day to walk the eight miles to the base, then two days on the face. After studying the guidebook and talking about what they'd do and what they'd need, the three lined up their food, gallons of water, tens of carabiners, doubles of all sizes of nuts on the rack,

ASTROMAN, YOSEMITE   HANS HERR

sleeping bags, ensolite pads, jackets and wool hats, belay seats, belaying devices, harnesses, climbing shoes and sneakers, adhesive tape for their hands, a cup apiece (it would serve for both drinking and eating), and one knife.

Four days later they were back in camp, taking a rest day. They had gotten along famously. Steve was a tall, soft-spoken, laconic climber, responsible for dozens of meagerly protected 5.11 routes among the hundred first ascents he'd done around Tucson. Before he did any difficult route, Steve would think about it intensely and kinesthetically, even for weeks. Now Hugh and Steve agreed to do *Astroman* together.

En route, Hugh and Steve traded leads. Hugh never fell, but he did scrape and bloody his knees in the Harding slot. The two had brought an extra rope and hauled along a pack; the only irritant that day was that it bounced, swung around, and snagged. Containing food, water, clothes, and a sleeping bag, it was heavy, too.

They never even used the things they brought. They weren't on the route long enough. They smoked up it in five hours. They shocked themselves, they did it so fast. "Without the pack," they said at the top, "we could have done it in three hours."

After *Astroman*, Hugh noticed a big difference in the Californian's attitude toward the brothers from Pennsylvania. It wasn't so much in what was said, it was in his manner. He now asked straightforward questions, and the insinuation was gone.

On that same trip a young climber named Christian Griffith, the same age as Hugh, was in the valley. Griffith flashed the 5.12 *Crimson Cringe* and, like Hugh, was spoken of as a prodigy. Hugh, eyeing Christian as the young man strolled around camp, was jealous.

Steve, watching Hugh, thought it would be good for him to step back and get humble. He took Hugh to the Cookie Cliff, known for its technically demanding, delicate climbing. They approached a face route with thin holds, *The Void*, 5.11-plus. Steve knew that Hugh would find it difficult. It was the kind of climbing that was Hugh's weak point—he was best at powering up big holds on overhanging routes—and the kind with which he had the least experience. Hugh's EB climbing shoes, moreover, were worn; he would get no help from the rubber. This kind of climbing was Steve's forte, however, and he had done the route before.

Steve cruised the route. When it was Hugh's turn, he fell off the crux move several times. Then he bristled with determination and charged. He placed a foot high and rocked up on it, using momentum to help him stand without going over backward. He stretched far to the right, his left arm straight out to the other side. Then he swung down right, his weight coming fully on one finger. A blood blister the size of a dime appeared on the finger, but he completed the move.

Watching, and remembering Hugh's scraped knees on *Astroman*, the easygoing Steve thought, "This guy has no respect for his body. I hope he keeps himself in one piece."

The valley regulars came to know Hugh—and his curious humor. One day Hugh came back to camp after a failed effort to climb a certain crack. His hands were raw, chewed to pieces. As he approached a few Arizona climbers, someone asked, "What happened to *you?*"

Stone-faced, Hugh said, "I was soloing, and I fell off and landed in a pit of lions."

———— • ————

The autumn he was seventeen Hugh wanted to go beyond what had been established in the Shawangunks. He had grown up during an era in which many of the best climbers, those at the leading edge, were doing bold routes for the challenge and the purity of the experience. Henry Barber had pioneered climbs that were not to be led again for ten or fifteen years. They became his trademarks. He and such British climbers as Ron Fawcett and John Redhead had established routes that were not only technically hard but minimally protected as well. Such routes were as taxing mentally and emotionally as physically. They required precise, creative engineering skills—the ability to calculate the chances of falling, and to make the best possible placements with small or insecure pieces of protection. Such routes required faith, commitment, a sense of adventure, and calmness.

Although Hugh made many well-protected severe ascents, he become known for his accomplishments on the hard and gutsy climbs. One such challenge, in the Gunks, he first heard about from a California climber. Dick Cilley had complained that the area guidebook author wouldn't write up a new route he had done because it was a toprope problem.

"Can it be led?" Hugh had asked.

"There's no protection, and it's really, really hard. If you try to lead it, you'll die," Cilley had replied stoutly.

Now, Hugh went over to the route and deliberately, strongly climbed up. His arms never did get overly pumped, and so after ascending what he would later name *Silly Dickens*, he went straight down the cliff and tried an aid route, *The Man Who Fell to Earth*. Hugh fired up and renamed it *The Boy Who Pumped to the Skies*. He had established two new 5.12s in one day.

But it was the day he did *Sticky Bun Power* that was the beginning of a new era in the Gunks, a time of very hard climbing on very little protection. For one of the critical sections on that route, Hugh placed a nest of tooth-sized brass nuts, brand-named R.P.s, behind a loose flake. The moves were solid 5.12. "Can't be careless, can't be sloppy," he told himself as he climbed.

As the author of *Shawangunk Rock Climbing* would put it, at this point "the difficulty of the newer routes had clearly surpassed the standard set by the ascent of *Super Crack*." Hugh was in the forefront of a new generation of climbers, the first to progress beyond the mythical Steve Wunsch era.

John Bragg and Russ Raffa, two of the top Gunks climbers, showed up at the cliff just after Hugh had finished *Sticky Bun Power*.

"What's next?" Raffa asked, shaking his head. That was what everyone was wondering, both at the Gunks and among climbers across the nation.

The route's reputation was sealed when Wolfgang Gullich, one of the best climbers in Europe, almost died on it. Pulling over the crux bulge at about thirty feet, he fell. His pieces of protection popped out of the flake, and he nearly hit the ground, which was covered with talus rocks.

Condemned Man was Hugh's hardest, most dangerous route: two pitches of 5.12 climbing on marginal gear, two pitches on which you could get yourself killed. Russ Clune named that route; Morris Hershoff named most of Hugh's others. Hugh wasn't into thinking up the routes' titles. He just climbed them. After one climb was done, he would be on to the next. Clune called Hugh "the boldest climber I've ever seen. He'll risk a ground fall on very, very hard moves."

45

And though such routes were certainly very dangerous, Hugh's approach was more deliberate than people usually realized. His method was to make many calculations, making sure the probabilities were in his favor. He would take every conceivable technological advantage. He might trail two ropes as he climbed, one clipped into numerous R.P. nuts, the other into different pieces of protection located lower down or perhaps off to the side. He viewed the tiny nuts in terms of safety in numbers: at least one, he calculated, would hold him if he fell.

Hugh later returned to repeat *Condemned Man*. This time, when he tried the hard moves, he fell. Eight of his ten R.P.s pulled out. "O.K., that climb, I admit, was a little out there," he said afterward. "But the important thing is that *two* held."

Since then, the route has seen only one repeat lead.

Hugh's nickname was the Boy Wonder, or sometimes Baby Huey, after the cartoon character who doesn't know his own strength. He was five feet eight inches and 135 pounds, with massive shoulders and arms. He was acknowledged to be the best climber in the Gunks, perhaps the East.

The inherent risks of the sport inspire many rock climbers with a macabre sense of humor. But Hugh's humor was muted. He was very serious. "I have to be," he reasoned. "To do those routes and stay alive, I have to be very, very serious." He thought of himself as a strange, detached youth.

The autumn of 1981 was one of the best times of his life. At the end of the season, when it was getting cold, he rappelled down to have a look at an old aid route, *Twilight Zone*. He was sure that it was harder than anything yet attempted in the Gunks. That would be his first project next spring.

Hugh moved around the house, finishing his packing for a weekend of ice climbing in New Hampshire. He was ready to go when his father asked him what mittens he had. John Herr dug into his own closet and produced his thick down ski mittens.

"Here," he said. "Take these."

"Great," said Hugh. "Thanks."

He drove to his friend Jeff Batzer's house, where both boys went to bed early, ready for a midnight start. They wanted to arrive at Mount Washington early enough the next day, Friday, to be able to do some reconnaissance before climbing Saturday morning.

Jeff, twenty and also from Lancaster, was a tool-and-die apprentice and competitive cyclist as well as a climber. The two young men had been to Mount Washington together the year before, in January 1981. They had had a good trip, climbing Pinnacle Gully in Huntington Ravine.

Both were extremely fit, and good rock climbers. Jeff's mountain experience consisted of only that previous trip to Mount Washington. Hugh's mountain background included his Bugaboos trips and the mountaineering forays of his younger years. In fact, he guessed he probably had the youngest ascents of a number of mountains in North America, such as Mount Temple in the Canadian Rockies at age nine, and peaks in the Cascades of Washington and the Selkirks of British Columbia. As he'd grown older, the mountain routes had become more technical; at age thirteen, he and Hans had climbed the Exum Ridge of the 13,766-foot Grand Teton in Wyoming.

The Herrs had also made several unsuccessful attempts. They had turned around in the face of storms before reaching the summits of Mount Victoria in Canada and Long's Peak in Rocky Mountain National Park, Colorado.

Now that Hugh was so focused on rock climbing, he would have preferred to be doing that, but it was the middle of winter. Ice climbing was a good substitute challenge, and there was satisfaction in the prospect of returning to the mountains. He and Jeff had been planning this trip for some time.

Jeff had first considered doing Pinnacle Gully, which he and Hugh had climbed before, as a roped solo. In anticipation of a solo endeavor, he had purchased a new parka, plastic boots, and other gear. But eventually he decided that it would be wiser to go with a partner and asked Hugh.

"Rope soloing would take too long," he thought. "Maybe I'd be up there too long." They would climb together.

Jeff's father was reluctant to let his son go out the door that night, even though he'd taken many climbing trips before. "Be really careful," said his father. "The weather's supposed to be bad."

In New Jersey the pair drove two and a half hours in the wrong direction, so the usual twelve-hour trip took them seventeen hours. Everywhere they went, it seemed that people—gas station attendants, store cashiers—were annoyed and angry with them. They had only two cassettes and ended up playing one by the Police over and over:

> *Sending out an SOS*
> *Sending out an SOS*

During the long drive, Jeff thought about reaching the summit of Mount Washington. He wanted to appear talented and successful in the eyes of climbers, his friends, his parents – everyone, really. He dreamed of one day being featured in *Climbing* magazine, or *Mountain.*

As a bicycle racer, he was in top shape now, better than he had ever been. After two and a half years of rock climbing, he wanted to start moving into the very different realm of mountaineering. He felt that he was better suited to it, that he was built for endurance, for pressing on while carrying a heavy pack. He didn't want to leave steep, technical rock and ice behind, but he did want to aim toward climbs above 20,000 feet and see how beautiful the world looked from up there.

Jeff knew that mountaineering, with its cold, snow, and avalanches, was far more dangerous than rock climbing, which is usually done in warm weather, but he simply felt more comfortable on a mountainside than on a steep wall. On a snow slope, he felt that he had his feet under him.

He wanted to build up a good resume of mountain climbs. He hoped to climb Rainier and maybe McKinley, then someday to get on an expedition to the Himalayas. Maybe Mount Everest, even . . . But Mount Washington would be the place to start.

"Hugh," Jeff said at one point, "I'd really like to get to the top this year."

Mount Washington, at 6,288 feet, is the tallest mountain east of the Mississippi River and north of the Carolinas. A wide, sprawling massif encircled by loose, skirtlike geologic folds, it would appear to be an easy mountain to climb. During many months of the year it swarms with people, its auto road overrun with vehicles. The mountain, part of the verdant White Mountain National Forest, is just a three-hour drive from Boston. A cog railway, built in 1869, runs some 60,000 people a year up one side of the mountain, and an auto road takes nearly 150,000 up the other. At the mountain's top, visitors can buy lunch and souvenirs in the Sherman Adams House or explore the nonprofit Mount Washington Observatory.

But in winter this peak is a formidable prospect; its list of fatalities likens it to mountains three times its size. Since 1849 more than a hundred people have died on Washington and its neighbors, mounts Adams, Clay, and Madison. Washington has claimed the lives of not just inexperienced outdoorspeople but even seasoned alpinists like Daniel

MOUNT WASHINGTON   DICK SMITH

Doody, a veteran of an Everest expedition, and Craig Merrihew. On a cold and windy March day in 1965, the two fell several hundred feet from Upper Pinnacle Gully, part of the fifteen-hundred-foot Huntington Ravine on the northeast side of the mountain, to the rocks at the bottom. They slid to a stop still tied together, with a bent ice screw dangling on the rope between them.

On Washington a teenager was once crushed by a collapsing snow arch, another was struck by a falling stone, a pair of climbers were caught in an avalanche, one hiker fell fifty feet after slipping on an icy rock, another fell sixty feet into a watercourse. More than twenty people have died in falls or "sliding falls"; a similar number have succumbed to exhaustion and exposure (five of them on or near the summit). Seven have drowned in the cold rivers and floods, and a few others suffered fatal strokes or heart attacks.

Most of the mountain's victims were hiking; others were climbing, skiing, snowshoeing, even following traplines. The remains of one long-ago victim were recovered after six years; two others were never found at all. The last time Hugh and Jeff had been there, on New Year's Eve, a climber had died in the mountain's Odell's Gully.

The primary reason for the disproportionate number of fatalities is the weather, considered as extreme as any on this continent south of Alaska, even as extreme as that of Antarctica. Aside from its location in the heart of a bitterly cold state, Mount Washington lies at the junction of three major storm tracks. One is the classic northeaster that comes up the Atlantic coast, another follows the Ohio River valley, and the third follows the St. Lawrence River valley. Although the storms rarely occur at the same time, they all generally head toward New England, where Mount Washington stands directly in their path.

Winds average 44 miles per hour on its summit, where the observatory frequently gauges velocities over 100. In 1934 the station clocked a gust that hit 231 mph, the highest recorded wind speed in the world. The winds are hurricane force an average of a hundred days a year. The average daily temperature is sixteen degrees Fahrenheit. The winter averages are nine degrees in December and five degrees in January and February, with highs of about thirteen degrees and normal lows of three below zero.

It was still light when Hugh and Jeff pulled off Route 16 into the parking lot at Pinkham Notch, site of an Appalachian Mountain Club camp and lodge, at the base of the mountain. The air was clear, and they could see all the way to the summit. They said only, "Look at that," and breathed deeply as their eyes scanned the mountain's broad flanks for several moments.

Then Hugh said, "Let's go."

It was a two-and-a-half-mile approach up a trail to the Harvard Cabin, the AMC hut where climbers frequently stay. With Hugh leading the way and both of them exhaling clouds of white, the two hauled their gear up the mountain. The trail twisted and turned among trees and rocks; the snow underfoot varied from hard pack, crunched down by many boots, to soft spots and then stiff windslab. Along the trail's wooded flanks, thin brown weeds stuck out from the white.

Swinging open the cabin's board door and entering, the two saw lights and a wood stove, seven other climbers, and Matt Pierce, the hut caretaker.

After greeting the boys and giving them a chance to take off their packs and warm their hands, Pierce said, "I know it's a bad subject, but do you have your money? It's six dollars a night."

"Uh-huh," muttered Jeff, not really paying attention or understanding.

A few minutes later, when they were upstairs settling in, they heard a voice from below. "O.K., you guys. I asked you nicely once before about the money."

Jeff caught on then. He poked his head down the stairway. "I'm sorry, I didn't realize you were talking to me," he said. "We left our wallets in the car." The year before, they hadn't been asked to pay when they stayed here.

"We'll pay on the way out," said Hugh.

Pierce, tired of climbers' ways, wasn't so sure, but there wasn't much he could do.

The two chatted a little with the other climbers. When they said they usually climbed in the Gunks, one of the climbers, who had heard Jeff address Hugh by name, said, nodding, "Oh, you're Hugh Herr."

Hugh was getting accustomed to such reactions. Now, not just in the Gunks but in other areas, too, people seemed to know who he was. His record in the Gunks and news of his trip to Yosemite had gotten out, and Henry Barber's comments had gone far. At Seneca Rocks in West Virginia, people had approached him. Or he'd hear them talking: "Look at that kid . . . Is that the one?"

Hugh and Jeff woke at dawn—seven o'clock—the next day. They could see out the windows that it was already snowing, and the summit was socked in, invisible.

Jeff assumed at first that they would not go out. He was crushed. "Man, if we don't do it now, we'll probably have to wait a whole year," he said. Nonetheless, the two slowly stuffed one pack with technical gear, and another with a sleeping bag and bivouac sack. They were appropriately dressed for a day out. Each put on long underwear, layers of wool clothing, Gore-Tex parka and outer pants, and mountaineering boots covered by padded Supergaitors.

Pierce was just posting the morning weather report as the two headed for the door around eight o'clock. The summit temperature was nine degrees Fahrenheit, and high winds and rapid weather changes were expected.

"What about avalanche conditions?" Hugh asked Pierce.

"There's only one gully that doesn't have avalanche danger now," Pierce said. "Odell's."

"Then that's where we'll go," said Jeff, "and check it out." He was thrilled to think that they could do something after all, rather than just hike or sit around all day. Pierce warned them and the other climbers that a big storm was expected.

Although Hugh and Jeff had talked in the car about the possibility of going to the top of the mountain, neither said anything about that now. They did not intend to be deceptive. But in an unwritten code that is part modesty, part self-protection (don't talk about it until you've done it), climbers are often reticent regarding their aims.

The boys said only that they intended to descend by the Escape Hatch Gully. Trooping toward the door, they were the first climbers out.

Snow fluttering around them, Hugh and Jeff hiked about three-quarters of a mile to the base of Odell's Gully, a branch of Huntington Ravine. Here, water seeping from a plateau above had formed a long blue ice runnel; the route would involve about five hundred feet of technical ice climbing and an equal distance of snow hiking.

Talking as they hiked, the two decided that the pack containing the sleeping bag would slow their progress. Hugh remembered how the pack had slowed him and Steve Grossman the summer before, when they had made their quick ascent of the eleven-pitch 5.11 *Astroman* in Yosemite. He wanted to go fast and light, alpine-style, a mode that was just beginning to gain popularity. The two elected to carry only technical gear on the climb and dumped their bivy gear at the base of Odell's Gully; it could be easily reclaimed during the descent. Their plan was to hurry to the top of the gully, then retreat.

They scrambled to the base of the route proper, to where the ice reared upward. Most of it rose at an angle of about sixty degrees, but one section of about ten feet went straight up. Jeff uncoiled the rope and stacked it in ready loops. Hugh started leading up the fifty-five-degree ice walls, moving fast and confidently.

An ice climber usually protects himself by threading his rope through carabiners clipped to ice screws inserted six to eight inches into the frozen waterfall. As in rock climbing, the stationary partner belays, and if the leader falls, he will drop twice the distance since his last piece of protection.

Hugh, however, decided to solo Odell's. Normally a soloist drags no rope, but he trailed the line for Jeff, who did not belay him. At the end of each rope length, he tied himself into ice screw placements to belay Jeff. Neither spoke beyond a few shouted rope commands.

"On belay!"

"Climbing!"

About 250 feet up, Jeff took off his right mitten and attached its strap to a Velcro closure on his sleeve while he fiddled to remove a stubborn ice screw Hugh had inserted for the belay. When he reached again for his mitten, it was gone, the closure pieces dangling. He wasn't too worried, though. He still had a silk vapor-barrier glove with an angora undermitt that was cut off halfway up the fingers to allow dexterity.

The two steamed up the four ice pitches in an hour and a half, then began to trudge through the loose snow above. The snow was dry enough that it did not ball up between their crampon spikes.

Hugh was worried about avalanches; massive walls of virgin snow loomed overhead. To avoid the danger, Hugh led well to one side of the gully, hugging the edge. The two were at the top of Odell's by ten o'clock.

The mountain's summit was eleven hundred feet higher, and just over a mile's hike. The boys crouched behind a boulder, out of the wind. Hugh felt safe for the first time since the two had begun climbing. They were in less danger now, on the relatively flat ground. Hunched over, hugging his knees, he thought about the conversation he and Jeff had shared during the drive. Should they go all the way up, or start down from here? It was time to decide.

When climbing, the two had always shared a teacher-pupil relationship. Now something in Hugh wanted to maintain that image. Within him was a subconscious memory of the days when he was the novice, determined to keep up with his older brothers in the mountains. He liked climbing with Jeff and wanted to climb with him more often. If Jeff wanted to reach the summit, Hugh wanted to get him there.

Hugh had no interest in getting to the top himself. Like many climbers more interested in technical difficulties than in summits, Hugh had cared only about doing Odell's. The hiking above held no allure for him.

All these thoughts, which would normally have occurred in a linear progression, came to him in the second before he spoke. It was a crucial moment, a pivotal instant.

"Do you want to try for the summit?"

"Do you think it would be O.K. to go on?" Jeff asked, feeling concern over the weather but still some hunger for the top. "Think we could make it?"

"Well, we could just go a ways, and maybe . . ." Hugh suggested. "If the weather gets worse, we can turn back." He was thinking that it wouldn't hurt to try.

Jeff reasoned to himself, "If he thinks we can go, it's probably O.K." Jeff had always trusted Hugh. Although he was still apprehensive, he

The Canadian border guard looked hard at the two boys on the Greyhound bus. "How old are you?" he asked.

"I'm fourteen," replied Hans. "My brother is thirteen."

The guard suspected they were runaways. "How much money do you have? Show me what you have."

Hans produced a hundred dollars and Hugh, seventy.

"You don't have enough money."

"We have more than enough," Hans protested. "We're camping."

The guard shook his head. "I can't let you through."

The boys phoned their father, who agreed to send them return tickets by overnight mail. That night, outside, they spread out their sleeping bags on their insulated pads. They had all the gear they needed to stay warm.

mainly felt encouraged: Hugh was going over the facts and was probably making a decent judgment. Sometimes Jeff watched Hugh do something frightening, such as a solo, and thought, "Oh, Hugh, don't *do* that," but he felt that Hugh always made decisions according to safety factors when the case involved the two of them. Hugh knew Jeff's limitations and was always respectful when Jeff had a hard time or got frightened on a climb. He would coax and encourage him, but if Jeff wanted to back off or be lowered, Hugh never argued.

"Besides," Jeff thought, "the hard part's behind us."

They agreed that they would start out, and then possibly sprint to the summit and right back down. It was cold and exciting, with ice crystallizing on their faces and the wind blasting around them.

"O.K., we're walking now. This isn't so bad," Jeff thought. "Visibility isn't so bad, we've got great equipment . . . the wind's really blowing but we're warm." He was delighted with his new clothing purchases. "This is fun. This is great."

But they had trekked upward only a few hundred feet when the visibility dropped to less than thirty feet. The wind was blasting at sixty-four miles per hour and gusting to ninety-four; the temperature was one degree above zero. The two had to keep shouting to each other to prevent being separated.

When they finally stopped at a knoll, the two thought they were probably at the summit, or very near it. By now Jeff didn't care much. "Things are starting to get out of hand," he thought.

"Let's get out of here!" shouted Hugh. He turned. On the way up, the wind had been blowing over their left shoulders; now they turned to face it on descent.

"O.K., we're going down now," Jeff thought. "This'll be O.K., this is fine." Trudging along, Jeff noticed some parallel marks in the snow. "That looks like the kind of tracks those machines make at ski trails," he thought. He never thought that the two were crossing the auto road that cuts a switchback up the mountain's north side to the top.

Though Hugh was just ahead, Jeff could hardly see him. "Hugh! Slow down!" he shouted.

"Hey!" Hugh called back eventually, staring down into a wide trough. "I think this is Central Gully!" He remembered it from the approach. Elated, he started run-stepping down it. Jeff could barely keep up.

"Slow down! Slow down!" Jeff implored, concerned that Hugh might slip on steep ice. Hurrying along behind, Jeff felt confident that they would soon be in Huntington Ravine. "We pulled it off," he said to himself.

Still above treeline, the two could see nothing of the terrain around them. It was late afternoon. The gully kept going, and going, and Hugh started to worry. Still, he knew that starting back up in such conditions would have been death, that getting into the shelter of the trees was the only thing that could protect them.

When the ravine flattened out into the forest, the two came upon a stream. Hoping it was one of the tributaries of the Cutler River, which runs into Pinkham Notch, they began to follow its banks. In fact, they were on a branch of the Peabody River and were going north, not east.

When they had abandoned their attempt for the summit, the boys had not considered the changeability of Mount Washington's winds. Their descent was actually of the mountain's northeast ridge, not its southeast, as they had thought. They had unwittingly entered the vast wilderness appropriately known as the Great Gulf.

What they did know was that they were now in trouble. They stripped the straps from their crampons and tried to tie them to branches to fashion snowshoes. But frantic that daylight was fading, they spent only ten minutes on the effort before abandoning it to hurry along.

The boys dumped their hardware and crampons and slogged along the riverbank. At first they were plodding through a foot of snow, but within an hour and well into the woods, they were struggling in drifts up to their waists. Sometimes they even floundered in chest-deep snow, forced to make swimming motions. Fir trees, their branches interlocking, further slowed their progress. Wherever the limbs met the snow, the boys had to crawl under them. Daylight faded away.

Too tired to fight the trees, they were forced closer to the river. But they couldn't see through the ice and snow to tell whether they were stepping over water or land. Twice Hugh broke through into water up to his shins. Now it was dark.

7

Matt Pierce, caretaker of the Harvard Cabin, became concerned when the boys had not returned by nightfall on Saturday and hiked out to the base of Odell's to call for them. Visibility was only fifty to seventy yards even with a headlamp, and the wind was blowing fifty miles an hour.

Around seven that evening, he made a radio call to Misha Kirk at the Appalachian Mountain Club hut in Pinkham Notch. "We've got two climbers overdue," he said. "They were going to climb Odell's and come back by the Escape Hatch."

Kirk, a thirty-one-year-old paramedic for the AMC, was not alarmed at first. People were often late getting back from their days out on the mountain. Still, he went through the standard motions, contacting the New Hampshire Fish and Game Department, the United States Forest Service, and the Mountain Rescue Service in North Conway. These agencies began their organization efforts immediately. Sergeant Carl T. Carlson of the Fish and Game Department called six officers who would be available with snowmobiles. Bill Kane of North Conway promised ten to fifteen volunteers. Two forest rangers, five volunteers from the AMC cabin, and five AMC employees joined the roster. It was too dark to start a search that night, especially in such weather, so the operation was slated to begin at six-thirty the next morning.

———————•———————

The boys were huddled together, colder now that they had stopped moving, shivering uncontrollably.

Hugh broke the silence. "If we don't keep moving, we'll freeze," he said.

"Let's keep going," Jeff agreed.

"I once read a story about a man who saved himself from freezing by walking all night," Hugh added.

They continued to hike until perhaps one in the morning. Then they found a granite boulder they could use for shelter and began to cut spruce branches to lie upon and under. Hugh was exhausted, his clothes soaked and frozen. He would cut a few twigs, then sit and stare, so Jeff collected most of the branches. Once they had crawled inside and were out of the wind, they weren't so cold. Hugh stripped his wet clothes off from the waist down and put on a pair of Jeff's wool cycling tights and socks before pulling his own wool pants back on.

That night they kept fairly warm by hugging each other, lying face to face with their legs interlocked. Sometimes they sat up and rubbed each other's feet for an hour or two at a time. They slept, but only a little.

"Stay awake," they told each other. They were afraid that if they fell asleep, they wouldn't wake up.

———————•———————

On Sunday morning Misha Kirk awoke at three o'clock, thinking he would begin early. He put on a headlamp and started out into the raging blizzard, up the trail to the hut, and then moved farther along, into Huntington. He arrived at the boulders lining the base of the Odell's headwall and saw something green partly hidden by snow. He slogged toward it, fearing to uncover a body, but cleared away the snow to find only a pack. In it were a sleeping bag, bivouac sack, and camera.

Below, the twenty or so rescuers began the organized search. They reasoned that the missing climbers could be injured and stalled anywhere along Huntington Ravine. The searchers would begin with the most probable areas.

Paul Ross, a member of the North Conway Mountain Rescue Team, took charge. Ross and a partner rode five miles up the mountain's auto road in a Thiokol snowcat, then set off and walked a mile farther, heading for the plateau known as the Alpine Garden, located below the mountaintop. They intended to descend from it into Huntington. But visibility was near zero and the winds were so bad that he and his companion spent more energy fighting to walk than searching for anything. Below them, some volunteers moved up into Huntington and Tuckerman ravines.

———— • ————

Hugh and Jeff found that their feet had swelled in the night. The boys could barely get their frozen leather boots back on. The snow continued, and a cold fog had rolled in.

"If we could just find a trail, we could walk right out of here," Jeff said as they crawled out into the snow.

Hugh didn't answer; he felt despondent. "If we don't get out today, it's all over," he thought. Talking expended extra energy. It was time to concentrate on survival.

The two boys struggled along through the drifts for hours in silence, not so much cold as filled with a bone-deep weariness and a numbing dread of the night. Hugh remembered how in his younger years he had thought a lot, and very romantically, about death. He had envisioned it in terms of an Indian taking a deep breath, expanding his chest, and then walking off into the forest to die. That image returned to him now. Inhaling deeply, he thought, "This is it."

Hugh said suddenly, "Look, we have a lot of clothes here, but not enough for the two of us. Instead of us both dying, let's split up and leave one behind, so the other gets all the clothes and survives." At the moment, his logic seemed brilliant, if frightening.

"It's my idea," he thought, "so I'm the one who should be left behind.

But that's the way it should be, since Jeff is going stronger." He stood there, waiting for an answer. Jeff just gave him a sideways look and said nothing. He hadn't accepted the idea of death at all.

As Hugh waded along, his shivering began to lessen. He felt merely cool, as if he were trying to sleep in the Gunks in a thin sleeping bag on a night when the temperature dipped near freezing. He guessed that it was now a little above freezing, never suspecting that he was about forty degrees off.

That day Hugh fell into the stream again, breaking through to his chest this time. The water, two feet beneath the ice, surged over his knees. He had a vision of himself being pulled under the ice.

"Jeff, help! Quick!"

Jeff darted a hand out to grab a tree and with the other extended his axe toward Hugh and pulled him out.

They kept going, not speaking. The snow reminded Hugh of a nice blanket, soft and thick and alluring. Exhausted, he wanted to lie down and give up. He would take two steps and have to stop, two steps, stop.

Hours later he spoke up suddenly. "Look, Jeff, a bridge!" They had been searching for the wooden spans made by trail crews to cross the water. Jeff stumbled forward and saw it was only a fallen tree.

Half an hour later, Hugh said, "There's a bridge!" Again, it was a log.

Twenty minutes later: "A bridge!"

Jeff looked and saw yet another log. "Hugh, cut it *out!*"

Hugh was either hallucinating or so desperate to see the bridges that he was conjuring them up. Ten minutes later he saw another but stopped himself from speaking. He looked away, then back. It was still there. He watched it carefully, suspiciously, until he was within five feet of it. Yes, it really was a bridge. Then both boys saw the sign beside it.

They had reached the junction of Madison Gulf Trail and the Osgood Cut-Off; signs pointed toward snow-covered trails to Pinkham Notch, the Mount Washington auto road, Madison Hut, and the Great Gulf Trail. It was about two o'clock Sunday afternoon.

"We made it," said Jeff. They both began to cry.

Studying the signs, the two looked for the trail leading to the closest destination, feeling they had no other choice. Pinkham Notch was four and a half miles away—too far, they thought, although the route would be downhill. They finally set off toward the Madison Hut, only two and a half miles away. Neither knew that this particular hut lay above treeline, about 3,300 feet above the stream; that its path was one of the roughest trails on the mountain; and finally, that the hut was closed in winter.

They flailed along the trail, sometimes crawling, other times clutching at trees to drag themselves upward. After struggling for two hours, they had covered barely a quarter of a mile. Finally, they turned back toward the intersection. As they neared the signs, Hugh collapsed. The snow felt soft and fresh on his face. Some slid down his collar.

He rose and was surprised to fall again, instantly. His brain couldn't deliver signals to his numb feet to adjust his balance, to stabilize his stance. As soon as his upper body tilted even slightly, he went down. He thought of a wooden toy he'd played with once, a figure with a small painted head atop its round body, and arms painted on its sides. The wooden man tipped over and sprang up, tipped over and sprang up. He fell again five feet farther, beside a boulder. This time he did not rise.

Jeff plodded over to him. "Here, let's get under this rock," he said. They were too exhausted to pull more than a few spruce boughs down before they crawled into the space where the boulder leaned against another.

They talked about home, of the spicy chili Hugh's mother made, of the iced tea that was a standard at Jeff's family's dinner table all year. The iced tea was no mundane fantasy: they were thoroughly dehydrated, dying of thirst. The thirst was far worse than the cold.

They tried to eat some bark. Then Jeff thought he remembered reading somewhere that it was poisonous, so they spit it out.

Their thoughts swung back and forth. Jeff thought of his family, with sweet visions of the dinner table that gave way to sad thoughts of letting his parents down. He thought about the chance that no one would ever find him, not even his body. He prayed out loud, in front of someone, for the first time in his life. "Lord, if you want us to get out, please rescue us." He wondered what would happen to his soul when he died.

Hugh, too, thought of his family, seeing them not in familiar situations, but imagining how each would take his death, feeling their horror. It was rather like realizing that a belayer below him was more afraid for his sake than he was. He saw them crying and pictured his father angry—both at Hugh and that the accident had happened. He felt not cheated but sad to die so young.

The boys could hear the water moving below the ice in the stream, just outside their shelter. Parched though they were, they could not rise. As evening approached, Jeff thought about the hole he'd seen in the middle of the frozen stream, but he knew he would break through if he tried to walk on the ice. Finally, he got up and made his way to the edge. Using nylon slings, he tied his ice axe to the end of a log, pushed the log out, and dipped his axe into the water. Like a sponge, a clump of snow on the axe blade absorbed the water. He ate the snow and dipped again for more. Twice he took shares up to Hugh before losing the energy it took to walk the three paces from boulder to stream.

At dusk Jeff tried to take his boots off, but something inside them stuck. The toes of his two pairs of socks had frozen rock-solid to the plastic. He finally inserted his ice axe into the boots and sawed off the ends of his socks. He then wrapped his parka around his stockinged feet while Hugh put mittens on his own feet. Hugh had felt fairly warm all day, but during the night he felt the cold acutely. The temperature had dropped to minus seventeen degrees, while the winds continued at fifty miles an hour.

———— • ————

When nothing beyond Misha Kirk's find had turned up by four o'clock Sunday afternoon, the search was suspended until the next day. The rescuers had exhausted many possibilities outside of Odell's, but because of the severe weather conditions they had not covered the entire gully itself.

The searchers knew only the missing climbers' names. Going through the boys' things in the hut that day, they had found the keys to Jeff's Datsun pickup. Two Fish and Game men took snowmobiles down to the parking lot, opened the truck, and then traced the registration.

The Batzers were called late Sunday afternoon and informed that the boys were overdue; they were advised to stay put until noon Monday.

At ten o'clock that night, Tony and Sally were coming home from a party. As Tony turned the key in the lock, they heard the phone ring. It was Hans; the boys were missing in a severe storm on Washington.

"I knew it," Tony thought. He turned to Sally and said, "It's happening." The waking dreams, the frightening fantasies, all the times he'd thought "What if he died?" flooded back to him. "It's real this time," he said.

He dialed the party he'd just left, knowing his parents were still there. When his mother came to the phone, Tony told her that Hugh was overdue.

Martha Herr was not terribly concerned. "Knowing Hugh . . ." she began. "Well, he's always inclined to make the most of any climbing trip, to squeeze in one last climb."

Later, Tony called his parents again, this time at their own home. "Have you heard anything more?" he asked. He heard voices in the background, and his mother joined in the laughter. His voice suddenly shrilled. "I hear laughter!" he said. "This is nothing to laugh about."

Martha tried to comfort him. "You know how those boys are," she said gently. "They're probably just getting in now. Let's just see what the morning brings."

Tony felt better. He went to bed right after the phone call, but then he lay awake, racked by a sense of responsibility. "I could have done more," he thought. "I could have prevented this." He had even wanted to go on this weekend trip with Hugh. In fact, he had been planning to, but since he had been away the weekend before, Sally had protested.

The next morning, when the boys still hadn't returned, Tony's parents knew the situation was serious. Tony came over to the farmhouse as they made quick preparations to leave. He was to stay there and man the phone.

At one point his father exploded in a moment of anger and grief. "It's just like you boys! You have some glorified image of dying on a mountain." He had been wanting to say that for years.

"You're crazy," Tony said, and walked out of the room.

Kelly's Run is a little green knob of schist along the shores of the Susquehanna River. The cliff is damp and mossy, and about its base are soft fronds of ferns. Fifteen feet off the ground, Tony and Hugh Herr were climbing.

"Tony!" Hugh gasped. His arms were burning with the lactic acid that comes from exertion. Tony reached down and wrapped one arm around his younger brother in an attempt to hold him to the rock. But now Tony's other arm was weakening, flaming out.

Screaming as they fell, the boys dropped off. Tony was still holding Hugh when they landed in the wet ferns.

In talking to his mother, Tony seemed more bewildered than anything else. "I don't understand this," he said. "Hugh has no interest in summits. I don't understand."

A little while later, thinking how much more time he spent in the mountains than Hugh, he told her, "This should have been me."

———— • ————

At dawn on Monday, Jeff tried to pull his first boot on and found the tongue frozen stiff. He pried both boot tongues open with his axe, but then his swollen feet rammed against the frozen clumps of socks within. He was able to dig the wad out of his right boot with his ice axe, then he and Hugh pulled together as hard as they could to force the boot onto Jeff's foot.

He worked on the other boot for two hours but couldn't get the sock out. He kept elbowing Hugh, saying, "C'mon, get your boots on." But Hugh would lean forward, pause, then drop back. His leather boots were caked thick with rime and ice.

Hugh hardly said a word, and Jeff thought he was delirious. But Hugh was simply thinking about dying and didn't have much to say.

Jeff finally gave up on his second boot and just put an overmitt on that foot. The boys lay still for a time, resting. Occasionally, they would mutter to each other, "O.K., we have to get out of this," then, a few minutes later, "We're gonna die."

Then Jeff sat up and crawled out. Hugh tried once more to get into his boots, gave up on them, and pulled his mittens onto his feet. He crawled out and tried to walk but could barely manage ten paces before falling over.

Jeff noticed that the fingertips of his right hand were white and hard. They did not hurt, only felt oddly wooden. Neither boy was worried about frostbite, though, only survival.

Jeff mustered his last reserves. "I'm going to try to get to Pinkham Notch for help," he told Hugh.

He started off, trying desperately to stick to the path. But the trail was buried under snow. He attempted to follow the orange blazes painted on trees to show the way, but the blowing whiteness stuck to the trunks and concealed them.

Several times he lost the trail but found it again. Then he lost it and couldn't find it at all. He was crossing his own tracks, reeling back and forth across the same area. Finally, he turned around and fought his way back to where Hugh lay.

"Hugh, I failed."

"That's O.K.," Hugh said simply.

"We won't try anymore."

"No."

Hugh relaxed totally then and let the cold engulf him. Completely numb, he felt neither hope nor pain. Fully accepting his death, he prayed that it come quickly.

Neither boy could stand now. Lying still, they lapsed into reveries.

"If God wants to get us out of here, he can," Jeff thought. "But I don't think that's gonna happen. I don't think we're gonna make it out."

Hugh thought about his friends at the Gunks, and all the routes he'd never do there. He thought about the intense pleasure he had always felt while in the Gunks, and how so many routes had been falling to him. Now he would miss everything.

He closed his eyes and waited for the great white tunnel he had read about.

————— • —————

The rescuers assumed that because Hugh and Jeff were so young, they were also inexperienced. With no way of knowing just how strong they were, or how great a distance they had quickly covered, the rescuers searched only those areas where the boys were known to have gone.

They hardly considered the possibility that the two had forged toward the summit. Almost no one goes clear up Mount Washington in winter after a technical climb. It's a cold walk up nondescript terrain, and in a storm there wouldn't be much to see.

On Monday morning, Paul Ross headed a Mountain Rescue team whose plan was to search the technical climbing terrain of Odell's Gully. He, Todd Swain, and Bill Kane stationed themselves at the gully's base with radios while two pairs of climbers set out. Doug Madara and Steve Larson started up the right side of the gully, while Michael Hartrich and Albert Dow took the left. The rest of the rescue team waited below, as support in case the boys were found.

Steve Larson had a problem right away. He had used his metal crampons for five years, but now, when he really needed them, spikes on not just one foot but both broke. Despite his abbreviated gear, he managed to keep pace with Madara, and the two went until they could see the gully's top ridge and be sure no one was lying there. They descended and rejoined Ross at the bottom.

Madara sustained minor frostbite, and he was hardly alone. Most of the searchers suffered similarly; all they had to do was face the wind and any uncovered fraction of an inch on their faces could freeze.

Hartrich, thirty, of North Conway, and Dow, twenty-eight, of Tuftonboro, were both strong ice climbers. Hartrich was a carpenter and former rock-climbing instructor, a quiet, honest, sometimes curmudgeonly New Englander. Dow was an instructor at the Eastern Mountain Climbing School, an open, cheery person. "Oh, God, it's cold!" he said with a muffled laugh from beneath his face mask.

Ice climbing was more like bulldozing than the fluid movements of rock climbing, but watching his partner's solid motions as they started up, Hartrich was reminded of his deliberateness on rock and reflected that he had probably never seen Dow out of control. Of all the climbers in North Conway, Dow seemed the most elegant whenever he was on rock, unerringly smooth and graceful. He had an uncanny sense of kinesiology, the ability to analyze moves, balance, and angles, and to share his understanding with students and colleagues.

When they neared the top of the left side of Odell's, the two found an abandoned carabiner and footprints leading up and out of the gully. They decided to follow the tracks across the Alpine Garden, then descend on the Lion Head Trail below it. They felt that walking over and down would be easier than rappelling in the high winds through the rock and snow slopes on that side of Odell's.

Hartrich had the radio, and Ross heard him say, "We're going over the garden." Then Ross could hear nothing more except static and a few garbled syllables.

Above, Hartrich and Dow struggled along, the wind knocking them off their feet. At times, they could see places where someone had stopped and made belays. But in the blowing snow, they lost the prints.

Ross switched to communication with the central board at Pinkham Notch. He kept asking, "Are they coming down?" He and his men were freezing but didn't want to leave in case they were needed. When he got a message confirming that the two were taking a different route back down, he and his group headed for the Harvard Cabin.

Also at the bottom of Huntington was Misha Kirk, who was startled by a sudden premonition.

"I think something's going to happen," he told his companions. "I think I better go up there."

Kirk's family had a history of extrasensory perception experiences. His Russian grandmother, a fortune-teller, was said to have stopped telling people's futures because she was so disturbed by her ability to predict their deaths. Misha's own mother had often dreamed things that came true. Once, when she was in Russia and Misha was in boarding school in Austria, he had become seriously ill. She called the school before administrators could call her. Misha himself had always felt he had a certain foreknowledge.

One of the men said, "They'll be O.K. You should come down to the hut and get warm."

"No, I'm going," Kirk said. He started skiing to the base of Lion Head to watch Hartrich and Dow come down. He traveled the two miles across, examining conditions. Looking up from the base of the trail, he could see that the storm winds had blown fresh snow into drifts on the mountain's eastern slopes. Up the ridge, on a steep slope, a cornice of new snow was perched on top of the old ice crust. It looked like the top of a three-scoop ice cream cone that was starting to melt in the summertime heat. Hartrich and Dow were heading down the ridge above it. If they proceeded onto the cornice, it could break and fall, dragging them with it.

As a member of the Pinkham Notch crew, Kirk was on a different radio frequency than the Mountain Rescue members; he could not communicate with Hartrich and Dow directly. He radioed to Pinkham Notch that the two should be warned of extreme avalanche danger and take every precaution, and waited till Pinkham Notch advised him that the message had been received.

THE STORY OF HUGH HERR

Hartrich and Dow had been nearing a fork in the trail. The branch known as the winter trail was used when avalanche danger was present. When they received Kirk's message, they cut over to the winter trail, deliberately picking the thickest part of the woods, where an avalanche was least likely to occur.

Hartrich was ahead, slogging among the birches, when something from behind knocked him forward. He was swimming in a tidal wave of snow.

———— • ————

The boys were hugging each other for warmth, legs overlapping. At intervals they would switch positions, giving relief to whoever had the bottom leg on the ground. Every time, they would knock knees and wince, groaning, "Oooo! Aaah!"

Pressure built up in Hugh's bladder. He held his urine, since he couldn't move. Then he thought, "I'm going to die anyway," and just released it.

Jeff, out of exhaustion and courtesy, didn't say a word, but Hugh knew he felt it. For a second Hugh even enjoyed the trickling warmth, but then that, too, became cold.

Enveloped and buffeted by white, Hartrich fought to stay afloat. He was dragged through a forest of birch and fir trees and felt some break as he hit them.

Finally a current of snow towed him down. As his body came to a stop, about a hundred feet from where he had been swept away, snow piled around his face. He made a fist and beat at the snow, popping out a hollow area around his head.

The snow immediately hardened; had he lain still, he would have been unable to move. With his one free arm he reached into his anorak pouch and retrieved the radio; he could not budge any other part of his body. He called for help. "This is unit four. We've been avalanched!"

He had last seen Dow a few feet above him and to his right. He waited, trapped, wondering what had happened to his partner. It was two o'clock.

In the Harvard Cabin, Bill Kane was trying to make radio contact. He, eight Mountain Rescue members, and two rangers heard Hartrich's voice come over the radio. Every man in the group raced over to Lion Head–some on foot, some in the rangers' Thiokol vehicle–to the place where the summer and winter trails converge.

The rangers dropped off the men, who immediately fanned out to search while the rangers drove south to the first-aid cache in Tuckerman Ravine for shovels and avalanche probes.

A two- to three-foot slab of loose snow, from south of the cornice, had avalanched off the thirty-degree slope. The sliding snow mass, approximately seventy feet wide and a hundred feet long, had caught both men.

Kirk assumed that when struck, Hartrich and Dow had been somewhere in the trees above him, between the summer and winter trails. Joe Gill, caretaker of Tuckerman's Cabin, joined Kirk in the woods. While they searched, they heard a "Whoomf!" as the snow settled six inches. It could go again at any time.

Kirk and Gill skied over to the avalanche debris area. There, Kirk saw the eeriest thing he had ever seen in the mountains: a single Dachstein mitten waving from the surface of the snow.

Hartrich was in the center of the avalanche deposition toe, and the snow was hard. Unable to free him without a shovel, Kirk took off his mittens and poked and dug out an airway.

It was now twenty-five minutes since Hartrich had radioed. In another twenty minutes, Kirk and Gill were joined by Paul Ross, Todd Swain, Steve Larson, and Doug Madara, who had been hiking down from the Harvard Cabin toward Pinkham Notch, and the rangers. They started the search for Dow with a coarse probe from the top of the gully, using twelve-foot poles to check the deposition debris and the below-surface snags. As they worked, the snow shifted again underfoot. Having made one pass down, they began a fine probe, standing almost shoulder to shoulder to comb the snow.

They finally found Dow, an hour and a half after the avalanche, six feet from where Hartrich had stopped. He had hit a tree: his back and the bones from his right shoulder to the center of his chest were broken. For half an hour Kirk and Bill Kane, one of the rescue service's three team leaders, attempted to revive him with cardiopulmonary resuscitation. Then they gave up.

A deep cut in his chin had not bled; he had died instantly. Other helpers arrived only to see Dow being brought down in a sled. Both Dow and Hartrich were taken to the AMC Lodge, where Dow was transferred to an ambulance. He was pronounced dead on arrival at the North Conway hospital two hours later.

Rescue team members drove Hartrich to the hospital, where he was checked and released. But the next day he could barely move. His whole body was bruised. The deep soreness would last for six days.

———————•———————

Only on Monday night, when the search was several days old, was Paul Ross able to learn much about the missing boys. Henry Barber phoned him. "Huey Herr is probably the best rock climber in the East," Barber said.

———————•———————

Hugh's parents were on the highway. They would drive for an hour or two, then phone Tony at home in case he had heard any news. When they crossed into New Hampshire on Tuesday morning, they stopped at a roadside diner. They parked right in front of a phone booth but in their distressed state never saw it.

John and Martha walked into the restaurant and noticed a man drinking a beer. "Why would someone be drinking beer first thing in the morning?" John thought distractedly. The man was sitting on a stool, his back to the Herrs.

A waitress approached, and John asked about a phone.

"Phone's outside," she said. Just then the seated man lifted his newspaper to read. John saw its headline: "Rescuer Killed in Washington Avalanche While Searching for Two Missing Climbers." He turned and walked out.

Martha had been right behind him. She had seen the headline, too. It had jumped out at her, looking like a huge banner. "That can't possibly be this rescue," she thought. As they walked back across the parking lot, she asked, "You don't think that could be the boys, do you?"

"I'm afraid so."

———————•———————

Back in Lancaster, the members of Hugh's gymnastics team learned from the Monday morning news that he was missing. A few of them heard it on the radio. They didn't know whether the situation was bad or not. They went to team practice that afternoon but did not accomplish much. "They've got good gear, anyway," said one boy.

On Tuesday the students heard more about the ferocity of the storm and the discovery of the boys' gear. Then they heard that a rescuer had been killed.

Though they didn't want to admit it, they now thought that Hugh was dead. Like many other teenagers, they had never known anyone who died. Not someone young, anyway, someone like themselves.

———•———

Lying still, Hugh and Jeff survived the third night. By Tuesday morning they knew they would not last another. Everything had happened so fast, Hugh thought, events coming at him as if he were in a car accident. It seemed as if he had been out here only a day.

He never thought there might be a rescue effort under way. He had been thinking in terms of getting to a road and phoning his parents.

All morning the two spoke little. About one-thirty Jeff heard the chopping sound of a helicopter at least five miles away and a thousand feet up. He crawled out and spread his red parka liner in the snow, hoping it would be spotted from the air. But the helicopter continued in the opposite direction. The sound faded.

———•———

An aerial search had begun. An Army National Guard helicopter, an olive drab UH1-V, known as a Huey, from the 197th EVAC in Concord, lifted off from Pinkham Notch at ten o'clock Tuesday morning. Although the weather had improved, the chopper still hit severe turbulence when entering Huntington Ravine, where, the rescuers believed, the boys were. The pilot was forced to fly as high as two thousand feet above the ground while the airborne searchers scanned the terrain through binoculars.

After one refueling stop, the helicopter resumed the search until its fuel supply again diminished. By three o'clock the search was over for the day, and the helicopter had returned to base.

The Herrs and the Batzers, now waiting anxiously at Pinkham Notch, had little hope. John Herr wasn't angry. He was heartbroken and gravely disappointed that his child's young life had been wasted.

———— • ————

The Mountain Rescue Service had not joined the search on Tuesday. It was not because of Dow's death, or the frustration, or the risk. The members simply believed that they had finished their job, having checked the likely areas as thoroughly as possible. But if the boys were found, they were ready to go back out and get them.

Bill Kane, representing the Mountain Rescue Service, spoke at an early afternoon press conference at the Eastern Slope Inn in North Conway. Around his eyes were dark patches of frostbitten skin. After the meeting a reporter asked, "What do you think their chances are?"

"Off the record," Kane said, "if they're up high—above tree line—I can't imagine they'd be alive."

———— • ————

In Lancaster, Tony had awakened that morning thinking, "I've lost my brother." He heard the phone ring and heaved himself out of bed to answer it.

"Don't give up hope, Tony," Morris Hershoff said. "There's still a chance. They could still be alive."

The morning passed dully into afternoon. Tony, Hans, Ellen, Beth, and Beth's boyfriend, Don Gallagher, huddled downstairs by the fireplace. They couldn't seem to get warm.

"It's all over," Tony was thinking. His brother and sisters seemed not to have accepted it yet. It was two o'clock. Light from the leaden sky barely lit the room.

"Let's burn the birch logs," he said abruptly. They all looked at the three pearly white birch logs stacked as decoration in a brass basket by the hearth. The three brothers had brought them home from a mountain trip to Ontario.

"Let's burn one," Hans said. "For Hugh."

In silence Tony placed the log on the fire, thinking he was sending his kid brother one last burst of heat.

"Maybe this'll get you through," whispered Hans.

———— • ————

Melissa "Cam" Bradshaw, twenty-eight, night manager for the Appalachian Mountain Club, was out snowshoeing in the Great Gulf on her day off. Just after one o'clock she came upon an odd series of tracks. Perplexed, she first wondered whether a moose had made them. Following the marks a short distance, she saw that they staggered and crossed themselves several times. She thought about the search and rescue effort under way on the other side of the mountain and decided to investigate further.

She had been following the tracks for an hour and a quarter when she heard a hoarse shout.

"Help!"

She snowshoed in the direction of the sound and peered beneath two rocks into a dark cavity. Amid snow and cut spruce branches lay two boys, side by side. Their faces were ashen, with cracked lips and sunken eyes that fixed on her with bleary gazes.

"Are you the guys from Odell's?"

"Yeah, that's us," said Jeff.

She crouched down, gave Jeff and Hugh water, raisins, a vest, and a wool shirt, and reassured them that she would return with help. But she was concerned about time, figuring that it would take her five hours to get back to Pinkham Notch. By then it would be dark.

As soon as she left, Jeff thought, "Boy I'm not sure we're gonna make it until the rescuers get here." He knew it would be at least two hours. "We've *got* to make it!" he thought then. He turned to Hugh, took him by the arms and gave him a little shake. He said, "We're going to get out of here! We can do it. If we just give it everything, we can live until they come." Hugh only muttered an affirmation, but Jeff knew he understood.

In fact, Hugh was wondering whether his own sense of relief was perhaps even more profound than Jeff's, since he had relinquished all hope while Jeff had never seemed to give up. They hugged again.

Jeff sank back. His thirst again overshadowed everything, even the possibility of dying. He couldn't stop thinking about iced tea.

———— • ————

Cam Bradshaw rushed off toward Pinkham Notch and the AMC Lodge. A mile and a half into the trek she came upon two men, Geoffrey May and David Boudreau from Massachusetts, who were on a five-day hiking trip. When she had passed their tent site earlier that day and waved, Cam had been the first person they had seen since Sunday.

Now she told them she had just found the two missing boys. "They're in really bad shape," she said. She directed the two men to go wait with the pair. "Follow my footprints," she instructed.

May and Boudreau pulled out their trail map and had her pinpoint the boys' location. After an hour-long hike, the two men heard Jeff calling and reached the niche. Using a foam sleeping pad as a stretcher, they dragged Hugh out and put him in one of their sleeping bags. They tried to give him water, but he drifted into unconsciousness.

As Cam started a two-mile run down the auto road, she met two AMC friends, Steve Johnson and Liz Lancaster, on cross-country skis. The two skied ahead of her down the auto road, reached Route 16, and flagged a car.

Back at Pinkham Notch, David Warren, the AMC hut manager, was conferring with the helicopter crew. The chopper had refueled and was about to leave.

Johnson ran up to Warren. "They're found and they're alive!"

The rescuers hastily began making plans and reorganizing. A few minutes later Cam Bradshaw phoned from a house on Route 16 with details of the boys' location.

———•———

Word of the discovery spread among the searchers and reporters milling around in the AMC Lodge. The Herrs suddenly saw people running in all directions across the parking lot.

John Herr stopped one of the hurrying figures. "What's going on?"

"Well, let's not get your hopes up," said the man. "We don't know for sure, but we got a report that two men were found. We don't know if it's your son."

"Just tell me one thing," John said. "Are they dead or alive?"

"They're alive."

———•———

At four in the afternoon there was a knock at the Herrs' farmhouse door. It was a reporter from Channel 8.

"Your brother's missing," she said. "How do you feel?"

Ellen took a step back. "How do you think I feel?" she said, trembling.

"I'm just doing my job," the reporter said. "You know that, don't you?"

"Please . . . please leave," said Ellen.

As she closed the door, the phone rang. When she heard Beth scream, Ellen thought, "He's dead."

Beth ran into the living room. "They found him alive!"

They all embraced and cried and danced.

———— • ————

Bill Kane, who an hour before couldn't imagine the boys would be found alive, now notified the rescue team to stand by.

Ten minutes after the AMC received the news from Steve Johnson, Littleton Hospital in Littleton, New Hampshire, was notified and asked to prepare for victims of hypothermia and frostbite. Ground crews, including Mountain Rescue member Misha Kirk, set off on foot along the Great Gulf Trail.

As the helicopter approached the site, one of the two hikers caring for the boys ignited a red flare. The helicopter crew members knew they couldn't land at the boulder because of the windy weather, rough terrain, fading light, and eighty-foot trees. Instead, the crew decided to hoist the boys into the craft. The pilot, Captain John Weeden, a Vietnam veteran with 43,000 hours' flight time, guided the helicopter to a hover just above a knoll a hundred yards from the flare. Here the trees were only twenty-five feet tall. Misha Kirk and another crewman, James Holub of the National Guard, lowered thirty-five feet to the ground on a forest penetrator hoist, a disk seat protected by metal phalanges.

Hugh awoke in what seemed like a pitch-dark room, with someone talking to him, asking him how he felt. At first he could barely speak. He had trouble when Misha Kirk asked him to count to five. Eventually he was able to tell Kirk that he felt sharp pains in his abdomen.

"That's a good sign you're coming out of it," Kirk said. He evaluated the boys' conditions. Both were hypothermic and frostbitten; Jeff could crawl, but Hugh was incoherent and would need to be carried in a litter.

It was a hot day in August, and the Herr children were playing out near the barn. Someone stumbled into a nest of yellowjackets. The children all scattered and fled—except Hugh, who at fourteen months was too young to run. By the time the older children thought to turn around and rescue him, he was staggering, draped in stinging bees.

Martha Herr wrapped him in her apron and rushed to the car. The little boy had taken two hundred stings, seventy in one arm alone; a ring of red welts surrounded one ear. Drugged by the insect poison, he began to fall asleep.

"Ellen!" cried Martha. "Keep him awake!"

Ellen shook him and rattled him and slapped his face until, at last, they reached the doctor's office.

Both of his legs were frozen from the knees down. One of Jeff's feet was frozen hard, as were the fingers on his right hand.

Captain Weeden and his crew decided they did not have enough fuel both to perform the lengthy hoist maneuver and to fly to the Littleton Hospital. The helicopter thunked away to Pinkham Notch to refuel. Misha Kirk stayed below with the boys and placed hot packs in their armpits and groins.

The helicopter, now refueled, returned at about five o'clock. After reviewing the situation, the rescuers decided that Jeff was lucid and mobile enough to be lifted in the forest penetrator. Geoffrey May, one of the hikers who had first arrived on the scene, carried Jeff on his back to the evacuation site. He struggled awkwardly on the steep terrain and in the three feet of fresh snow. At the knoll, Jeff was fitted with a harness and then lifted by the forest penetrator. He swung up and into safety at five-fifteen, as light slipped away. There was no conversation as he came into the chopper; there was no time.

Hugh now had to be lifted immediately or the helicopter mission would be aborted because of darkness. He would be hoisted in a Stokes litter, a body-sized steel-mesh basket, from where he lay. This plan would be more difficult to effect than carrying him through the snow to the knoll, but faster.

Captain Weeden flew in circles above the trees, waiting for Hugh to be packaged. More ground crews had arrived to help. At five-forty Kirk reported that Hugh was prepared in the litter. The helicopter hovered a hundred feet above.

All operations were now taking place under the beam of the helicopter searchlight. Within that yellow circle, head lamp beacons swung and stabbed. Rotor wash blasting up to a hundred miles an hour kicked snow into the light and rescuers' faces, abrading and freezing the skin.

In the back of the helicopter, Sergeant Walter Lessard lowered a cable to the ground while reporting the position of the helicopter to the captain and other crew members. Captain Weeden struggled to hold the chopper steady.

Many hands hauled Hugh to a boulder in the stream. From within his wraps and straps, he could hear people talking, hear the helicopter, feel the stretcher inching along. He heard someone say, "Don't let him fall in the stream." He was helpless, terrified.

He heard the clink of the helicopter's winch cable attaching to the litter basket. After Kirk tied draglines to the litter, Hugh heard people saying, "O.K., ease him out, ease him out." He could hear the tension in the men's voices. Then he was jolting and swinging in his basket.

The sleeping bag was so close around his nose that he could barely breathe. He heard someone say, "He's over the stream."

As the litter rose, the men pulled on the draglines to prevent it from spinning or veering. If it were to swing more than fifteen feet in any direction, it would get caught in the trees.

A hundred feet up, the litter revolved, its head catching below a helicopter runner. Lessard struggled and pulled but could not move the litter with his thick gloves on. Despite the icy temperatures and the two-hundred-mile-an-hour wind from the helicopter's rotors, he took his gloves off. He continued fighting with the basket for several long minutes. Then, suddenly, it slid in. It was five-forty-five.

The door shut, and for the first time in three days, Hugh couldn't hear the wind. Slowly, wonderingly, he thought, "The wind is outside and I'm inside."

The sleeping bag over his face pressed down more closely, cutting off his breathing. He started screaming. Four times he shouted, "Help!"

Then he heard Jeff's voice. He'd forgotten about Jeff. "Hugh, Hugh, we're going to live," Jeff said. "We're going to see our moms and dads."

One of the crew walked back and with a rough gesture lifted the bag off Hugh's face. Hugh thought drowsily, "He's sort of pissed. Something is weird." Then he slept.

When the helicopter began to descend, Jeff felt a wave of fear. He thought the craft was making an emergency or crash landing, but it was only stopping at Pinkham Notch to refuel. Ten minutes later it rose and continued. Peering ahead into the darkness, Jeff saw the lights of Littleton. They represented life to him. He stared at a huge cross on a hill, completely lit up.

9

The boys arrived at Littleton Hospital, which specializes in the care and treatment of frostbite victims, at seven o'clock Tuesday night, three full days after they were reported missing. From a parking lot lit by flashing ambulance lights, medics carried them into the emergency room.

Jeff's core temperature was ninety-four degrees, Hugh's, ninety-three. No one could tell how low their temperatures had been before they had received aid from the hikers.

Hugh was taken into a first-aid room equipped with a hypothermia blanket unit, blood warmers, heated humidified air, space blankets, and hot water. As medical personnel stripped off Hugh's clothes, his doctor, Campbell McClaren, and his parents stared at his blue body and thought he was completely frostbitten. But then the doctor touched his skin and looked at his own fingertip.

"It's dye," he said. Hugh's long underwear, wet by sweat and river water, had stained his skin.

Hugh's first discernible image was that of his parents' faces. He looked up and told them he loved them.

"We love you, too," they said.

Forty minutes later Hugh's feet were soaking in a tub of 104-degree water. Surprisingly, his hands were essentially unaffected.

Jeff, too, entered an observation room containing space blankets and a tub of hot water. Within minutes his hand-knit Icelandic sweater had been cut off and he was in the tub. His feet were not as frostbitten as Hugh's, but his hands were in bad condition.

Both boys were placed on cardiac monitors and given ampicillin and tetanus toxoid as prophylactics. Each hour they received infusions of Dextran, which expands plasma to improve blood dynamics, such as blood pressure and pulse rate.

Three hours after they entered the hospital, the boys were placed in the intensive care unit, and half an hour after that their temperatures had reached ninety-eight degrees. They were able to move their feet and toes, but the skin was badly discolored. Each was given morphine intravenously for pain in the extremities. Both had blood in their urine. That night they slept, never waking.

The hospital staff sent emergency guards to the ambulance dock and emergency room entrance to restrain the cluster of press people. The reporters were directed to the solarium, dining room, and front lobby.

Jeff's father eventually spoke to them. "I have three sons," he said, "and this morning I thought that I had two."

The next day, Jeff's feet blistered from ankles to toes. Hugh's feet were purple and cold. Only a few blood blisters rose on them.

Hugh's father called home to give another report. He spoke to Ellen, whose happiness flowed over the wires. He tried to caution her a little. "We're just starting to climb the mountain," he said. "We've got a long way to go." He thought Hugh might lose a toe, maybe two.

———— • ————

On Wednesday, after they realized they were going to live, the two boys learned that someone had died trying to save them. Jeff got the news as he sat in a whirlpool, when a nurse gently asked him if he knew that a man had died in the rescue effort. He broke down and cried. "We don't deserve to be here," he said. He immediately turned to prayer. "Lord, help me through this," he implored.

Hugh was alone, lying in bed, when a doctor told him about Albert Dow. He moaned, then cried.

That evening, the two boys wept together. Hugh recalled how he had pictured his own family in postures of grief, and he tried now to picture Albert's family in those same positions. Was Albert's father gray-faced, his features set, masklike? The mother's head against the father's shoulder? Did the father cry out when he heard? What were they doing this minute?

He felt an overall, pervasive disbelief. He wanted to jump back in time, to do things differently. To have another chance. He was enraged at himself.

He thought back on the precepts of clean, ethical climbing. Needing a rescue was the worst violation of clean climbing's ideology of independence, the most unimaginable mistake. Hugh, in fact, had never imagined it; he would have recoiled from the thought. And now the worst horror of all was that in needing to be rescued, he had caused the death of another human being.

He searched his motivations, the elements and layers of thoughts that had brought him to this point. Eyes closed, he acknowledged to himself his strong desire to be accepted and loved. Did those needs, he wondered, underlie the actions of every person who strives to do great things, who wants to be known, who desires power?

With a groan he thought, "Oh, my father is going to be so angry."

Now, John Herr walked into his son's room and said, "I'm proud of you."

Hugh was bewildered, then angry himself. "What are you talking about? This is awful."

Many others, too, seemed to treat the boys almost as heroes for being alive. Hugh found that unendurable. He withdrew, shut people out. He needed time alone in his mind, to confront the shame and horror. He lay in his bed that afternoon, that night, trying to sort through what had happened, to make sense of it. He could not.

Hugh's emotions shot up and down during hours that seemed interminable, during minutes that were overwhelmingly acute. Sometimes he felt pure bliss: he was alive, when only yesterday he had been certain his life was ending. But that always gave way to anger. Staring

Mount Washington fatalities caused by exposure, falls, and avalanches: 1849 Frederick Strickland • 1855 Lizzie G. Bourne • 1856 Benjamin Chandler • 1869 J.M. Thompson • 1874 Harry W. Hunter • 1886 Sewall E. Faunce • 1890 Ewald Weiss • 1900 William B. Curtis, Allan Ormsbee • 1912 John M. Keenan • 1927 Harriman • 1928 Elmer Lyman, Herbert J. Young • 1929 Oysten Kladstad • 1931 Henry B. Bigelow, Jr. • 1932 Ernest W. Mc-Adams, Joseph B. Chadwick • 1933 Simon Joseph, Rupert Marden • 1934 Jerome R. Pierce • 1936 John W. Fowler, Grace M. Sturgess • 1938 Joseph Caggiano • 1940 Edwin P. McIntire, Jr. • 1941 Louis Carl Haberland • 1943 John Neal • 1948 Phyllis Wilbur • 1949 Paul H. Schiller • 1952 Tor Staver, Raymond W. Davis • 1954 Philip Longnecker, Jacques Parysko • 1956 A. Aaron Leve, John J. Ochab, Thomas Flint • 1958 William Brigham, Paul Zanet, Judy March • 1962 Armand Falardeau, Alfred Dickinson • 1964 Hugo Stadtmuller, John Griffin • 1965 Daniel E. Doody, Craig M. Merrihue • 1969 Scott Stevens, Robert Ellenberg, Charles Yoder, Mark Larner, Richard Fitzgerald • 1971 Barbara Palmer, Betsy Roberts, Bowdoin • 1972 Christopher Coyne • 1973 Peter Winn • 1974 Karl Brushaber • 1976 Margaret Cassidy, Scott Whinnery, Robert Evans • 1979 David Shoemaker, Paul Flanigan • 1980 Patrick Kelley, Charles LaBonte, Peter Friedman • 1982 Albert Dow

at the white ceiling, he said slowly to himself, "Someone died in a situation that I created, but I am still here." He felt guilty and resented his very life. Sometimes he wanted to be still out there in the snow, left alone to die. "That seems fair," he thought, "and a lot easier than living."

When such pains came, he let them happen and didn't try to comfort himself. But somewhere in the back of his consciousness he also had faith that things would get better.

The anger and deep, deep shame only sometimes receded. The former would eventually fade, but the shame would always be there.

———— • ————

Hugh's calves swelled so much that his doctor made incisions into the skin and muscle to relieve the pressure and improve the circulation. Because the procedure was successful, Jeff underwent a similar operation.

During the first week of hospitalization, both boys continued to receive Dextran infusions hourly. Their urine cleared and their appetites began to return. Each was given injections of Reserpine in each femoral artery to relieve symptoms of high blood pressure; Jeff also received injections in each brachial artery because of the frostbite in his hands. Both were given 10 grams of aspirin daily as an anticoagulant.

Misha Kirk, Bill Hastings of the Fish and Game Department, and David Warren of the AMC visited them to hear the full account of what had happened so that they could complete an official report. Kirk arrived early, alone. The first thing Hugh asked him was, "Am I going to lose my feet?" It was a question he hadn't asked the doctors.

"I think you'll be O.K.," Kirk replied, even though he actually thought otherwise.

Jeff, who had talked to Kirk during the rescue, cried when he saw him, and hugged him.

Jeff's brother, asked by numerous reporters for an explanation of what had happened, said the two had gotten turned around when hit by a whiteout while they were in Odell's. He didn't say anything about their going to the top. He didn't yet know the full story himself. Many papers published his sketchy account.

Some papers came out with erroneous reports. One said the two boys had carried and shared a sleeping bag. Another said they had been found digging themselves out of the snow. Others said they had stayed alive by beating each other with branches.

The press set in. As the boys lay in the hospital, more than twenty media organizations requested interviews. Finally, doctors and patients agreed to a question-and-answer session.

The two boys were lying in beds side by side as the reporters came into their room. Jeff was keyed up and expressive – he was grateful to be alive, despite his sadness over Albert Dow's death, and found the talking cathartic – but Hugh was nearly silent.

"We were really psyched for the trip," Jeff said. "We only had two days to do something, and it might have been a stupid decision to climb but we wanted to do something.

"It's just great to be alive," he said.

Asked about what had happened, Jeff said, "I thought there was nothing easier than going up there and coming right back down." He didn't point to the mistake of going beyond Odell's toward the summit; the two hadn't thought all the events through yet. Jeff called leaving the pack "a big mistake." Of what ensued, he said, "We just got corkscrewed around."

Only one reporter, from the local paper, asked the difficult questions – about Albert Dow, and whether the boys had been prepared for the severe weather. The others simply asked what happened and, repeatedly, the same questions about what it had felt like to face the end.

When yet another reporter asked him, "What's it like to freeze to death?" Hugh replied, "So why don't you ask someone who has?"

He just wanted them all to go away. He hated the press attention, hated having this horrible thing he'd done publicized. He would rather have declined the interview, but it had seemed his duty to speak. To refuse after having just been rescued seemed wrong, ungrateful.

Several published photos showed a smiling Jeff in the foreground. In some shots he obligingly hugged his mother for the camera. In the background of those same photos is Hugh, expressionless, looking sideways at the camera.

Flipping through one of the newspapers, Hugh opened to a picture of Albert Dow. He froze, then pulled it closer and studied the face. That was when reality fully permeated the film of disbelief that had partly protected him. Something in Albert's face reminded Hugh of the open expression of Alex Lowe, one of Hugh's best friends.

Hugh learned that Albert was soon to be married, and he often thought about his fiancee. He knew that her name was Joan Rigley and that she was from Brownfield, Maine. He wondered what she was thinking.

Alone, he concentrated on figuring out his mistakes. The worst, he thought, the real one, was to continue out of Odell's. He did not see himself as a victim. "No," he thought grimly, "it was my own bad decision." Leaving the pack containing the sleeping bag in order to climb quickly did not even now seem unreasonable. Hugh had been doing many fast ascents, such as *Astroman*, and in making the decision he had been recalling how much a pack had slowed him and Steve Grossman on that route. When, on Mount Washington, he had chosen to go alpine-style, light and fast, he had reasoned that the less time he and Jeff were climbing, the less danger they'd be in from such hazards as storms, rockfall, and avalanches. Hugh had been anxious about the loose snow above them on the slopes of Odell's; he had wanted to get up and out of the avalanche zone as fast as possible. The difference was that on *Astroman*, he and Steve had wanted a faster time for personal gratification; here on Odell's, he had been hoping to increase his margin of safety. If he and Jeff had needed an extra thirty minutes to an hour to climb Odell's because they were carrying the pack, he thought, and had been hit by an avalanche during that time, then the mistake would have been to take the pack. The decision to leave the pack would have been right if he hadn't gotten disoriented. But it was wrong because he had.

Lying in his bed and thinking, Hugh realized that he had taken a rock climber's mindset into the very different arena of the mountains. Lately, in his climbing, he had been essentially ignoring his body; the sport to him had become entirely mental. He would focus on relaxing in critical situations, think his options through, and then move aggressively. He would plan so carefully that during an ascent he simply blocked his fear. On rock, with rope and well-placed protection, blocking fear had been the right thing to do. Logic and will pulled him through. But now he'd made a mistake in an arena where calmness wasn't enough.

Odell's hadn't seemed extreme at all; he'd had to solo the route to challenge himself. He'd been too relaxed. He had anticipated avalanches, he had anticipated falls, but he had never anticipated getting lost.

————•————

Two days after the rescue, Dow's body was cremated. More than five hundred people attended the memorial service at Melvin Village Community Church, on the shores of Lake Winnipesaukee. The churchyard was buried beneath four and a half feet of snow.

The Dow family had lived in nearby Tuftonboro for generations. Albert had graduated from Kingswood High School in 1971 and from the University of New Hampshire in 1975. He had been an Eastern Mountain Sports climbing instructor, a mountain rescue volunteer, and a member of the Waterville Valley ski team. He had been one of the stronger climbers in North Conway, able to lead 5.11 and put up new routes of 5.10 to 5.11-plus.

What people remembered most about him, however, was his warmth: his friendly, welcoming manner. When a newcomer came to the area, intimidated perhaps by the "hard men" among the local climbers, Albert was likely to be the first to try to set him at ease. One visitor to the cliffs mentioned shyly to Albert that he was thinking of moving to the area. "Great!" said Albert. "Join the party!"

Now the Reverend Greta Dow, his second cousin, presided over his funeral service.

"Occasions when a person has actually given his life in an effort to help someone else are rare," she said. "But Albert has given us a prime example of true, unselfish caring." She told the congregation that Albert Dow and Joan Rigley were to have made their engagement official on Valentine's Day.

———————— • ————————

Martha Herr was walking across the parking lot at the AMC lodge, looking for Cam Bradshaw and wanting to thank her and others, when she came upon Misha Kirk. He put a hand on her shoulder. "I want you to understand," he said, "that *we* do not feel this way about it."

"Oh," she said, confused. "Well, thank you." She didn't understand what he was saying until she read the newspapers the next day.

Charles Barry, the Fish and Game director, was quoted as saying, "I'm sick and tired of . . . committing people to rescue people who shouldn't have been there in the first place." Other sharp comments followed.

Major Joseph Riley of the National Guard said, "We will not sit back and place our crews in jeopardy to provide the press with a dramatic rescue spectacular."

Once the criticisms began to show up in the newspapers, they increased and spread. More observers joined in. The Herr parents didn't have enough information to understand what was happening. On the night of the rescue, the ground crew and rescuers and helicopter crew had shaken hands and seemed happy that they had saved the two boys. Now, the papers were running negative articles and editorials. Jeff's mother picked up a paper one day as she and Martha went to a laundromat. Joan Batzer read an article, then turned to Martha and said, "We have enough problems. We don't need this, too. We won't get any more papers. It just depresses us."

As much as anything, it was the apparent accumulation of errors that caused the perception that the boys had been cavalier and brash. A contributing factor was that at the Harvard Cabin, the boys were alleged to have been out for themselves – not having their money ready, not washing their breakfast dishes, not doing any chores other than stacking wood for the stove. In town, feeling ran high that a pair of arrogant flatlanders had come into the state, and one of its own had perished for it.

"Those little hot dogs thought they could get away with anything, and somebody lost a life because of it," a woman in North Conway said bitterly.

A rumor began in the North Conway climbing community that Hugh had said something callous about how Dow, being a volunteer, had been on Mount Washington by choice. But Hugh hadn't made the comment at all; that was what well-meaning people were telling him in an effort to console him.

Probably the incompleteness of the initial accounts given by the boys or their families—before they had fully considered events in retrospect—suggested to observers that the Pennsylvanians had not taken full responsibility for their actions. Additionally, some papers wrote only about the miracle of the boys' survival and did not discuss causes and effects. Residents were frustrated when published accounts didn't point out the mistakes the boys had made.

Now, with hindsight, those mistakes had been identified. The pair's decision to climb to the summit instead of retreating when the weather worsened got them lost. They did not disclose all their plans for the day, so rescuers looked for them in the wrong places. They ditched their bivy gear, which they could have shared in relative warmth. And although unfamiliar with the area, they carried no map or compass. The accident now seemed to be a case of many, many ifs, the end result of a string of factors.

Bradford Washburn, a respected mountaineer, argued that the AMC should have indicated on the trail sign that the Madison Hut was closed in winter. Though he faulted the boys for, among other mistakes, not recognizing the auto road when they walked over it, he said that their futile effort to reach a closed shelter "was the crux of the whole matter." He pointed to this incident as "a major factor in the seriousness of their frostbite. Maybe those boys couldn't have walked all the way to help, but they could have gotten a lot nearer to it than they were—and the girl who found them would have sounded the alarm much sooner."

People began to take sides. Many, especially those unfamiliar with mountaineering, pointed to the boys' decision to leave the pack behind. They did not understand the thought process behind that act; right or wrong, Hugh's intent had been to give Jeff and himself a better chance of safety. On the surface, it appeared as if the boys had rated themselves as so skilled that they would never need emergency gear.

Jeff's words – on that subject especially – had surely exacerbated the situation. His comments had been innocent, but Hugh disagreed with them. He thought that Jeff, who had had little mountaineering experience, had not understood all the reasons behind the decisions they had made.

What was final and incontestable, however, was the end result: Albert Dow was dead. And the boys were badly injured.

A lawyer, a former client of Dow's at the Eastern Mountain Sports climbing school, decided the school had a case against the two boys. He presented his idea in a letter to Joe Lentini, the head of the school, who had participated in the search. Lentini showed the letter to the members of the Mountain Rescue Service at their next meeting. They were taken aback and wanted nothing to do with initiating a lawsuit against fellow climbers. That seemed against all the tenets of mountaineering, with its sense of community, its freedom from strictures, its tradition of helping and caring for its own.

In the press, Misha Kirk acknowledged that the boys were "not as prepared as they might have been," but he also said, when asked how he felt about the death of a rescuer, "I was talking with my team on the way down Monday and we all said the same thing. If we go, we'd like to go that way – in the mountains, helping someone."

———— • ————

Hugh was hyperventilating. Between racking gasps, he screamed, "Nurse!"

A nurse entered his room, asking "What? What?" Her tone was impatient. She took his temperature: it was 105 degrees. Concerned about infection, doctors rushed him into surgery.

"If we can't get his temperature down, we'll have to do an amputation immediately," a surgeon told his parents.

The Herrs were not at all prepared to hear that. Hugh's feet were pink; he had been moving his toes a little.

Paul DiBello of nearby Conway, a young man who had lost his lower legs to frostbite after becoming lost on Mount Katahdin in Maine, had visited Hugh in the past few days. Now he introduced himself to Hugh's parents.

He motioned to Martha Herr to join him out in the hall. She followed him as he led, walking with deliberate steps, his upper body slightly forward and his knees and thighs seeming to move little. Outside, he said, "Don't let them save his feet." She looked at him blankly.

DiBello explained. "They always say save, save, save the tissue."

He was a tall, densely bearded, hard-faced man, apparently in his thirties. He seemed angry but forthright. And though his voice was rough, too, she had the sense of his compassion and wanted to hear him out.

He told her of his own history, when doctors had tried to avoid amputation. They removed one leg and tried to save the other. He was in and out of the hospital for three years, trying to walk and breaking down again and again; in pain, he became a drug addict. DiBello was bitter now about that period: he felt that a large chunk of his life had been ruined. In fact, many patients undergo thirty, forty, even fifty operations only to have their injured limbs amputated after all.

Finally, DiBello had told his caretakers, "I will not sign for any operation other than an amputation."

On the day after the amputation, he said to Martha, "I felt so good, I was up dancing with the nurses."

Though she understood his intentions to be good, Martha felt traumatized.

In the operating room, Hugh began vomiting blood mixed with the cranberry juice he had been drinking to help stave off kidney failure, and passing blood through the rectum. His physicians realized the problem was a potentially deadly ulcer. It had developed due to stress, the series of shots in the groin, and the massive doses of aspirin he had been taking. They were able to medicate him and avoid surgery.

As the days passed at the end of the first week after the rescue, Hugh noticed that some hospital staff members seemed gruff. He recalled the impatience of the nurse. His parents decided they had to tell him what people were saying. He just listened.

He began to receive mail criticizing him. It seemed there was a bad one in the eight or ten letters that arrived each day. Some of the letter writers were sympathetic; some expressed religious sentiments; but some told him he had made a big mistake and said they hoped he'd learned his lesson. One woman whose husband was a volunteer wrote, "It's people like you who get people like my husband killed."

His parents began screening the mail before they brought it to him. Hugh began to jump every time the phone rang.

Hugh, lying in bed, could see how people might read the events as a string of errors. Over and over he reviewed what had happened.

"Should we have carried a compass?" Hugh wondered. Most climbers heading out for a day trip of ice climbing carry no compass. There hadn't been much chance of getting lost while he and Jeff followed the gully and stayed within the ravine. Once they entered the featureless, relatively flat Alpine Gardens above Odell's, however, they would not have gone the wrong way – or could have righted themselves once they did – if they had had a compass.

"What about a map?" he asked himself. He recalled standing at the trail junction, reading the signs. "It wouldn't have mattered what trail we took that day," he thought. "The trail to Pinkham Notch was downhill, but we still would have failed to get anywhere because of exhaustion."

Every possibility, every argument kept returning to how they'd gotten into the situation in the first place. "Our mistake was to venture even ten minutes above Odell's without a compass," he concluded.

Hugh was ready to take full responsibility – personally and publicly – for that bad decision. He would not have flinched if an expert climber had criticized him. But he was disturbed to be represented as a flatlander who had caused an accident through youth and inexperience, especially by people who were not mountaineers.

"It was a misjudgment, an accident," Hugh thought. He felt he'd made only one mistake: to continue above Odell's toward the summit. "After walking the tightrope for many years, I slipped. After living on the edge for so many years, maybe it was inevitable that I would make a mistake."

———— • ————

Hugh's sister Ellen had arrived with Hans for a weekend visit. At first they were glad just to see their brother alive; it never occurred to them to worry about frostbite. But gradually the seriousness of his condition sunk in. On Sunday, when Hans had to leave to return to his work as a machinist, Ellen made a decision. "I don't have to leave," she said to her mother. "I'm staying. I couldn't study. I'd sit in class in Penn State and be seeing Hugh propped up in bed."

Hans left reluctantly. He avoided the North Conway traffic by by-passing town on the West Side Road, past woods and then fields. It was smooth and mainly straight, and Hans didn't know he was speeding until he saw the spinning blue lights of the police car that had pulled up behind him.

"I'm sorry," he told the officer. "I wasn't concentrating. I just came from seeing someone at the hospital." The policeman read the last name and address on Hans's driver's license and registration and gave him a look of compassion.

"I understand," he said gently. "Drive safe. You've got a long way home."

Ellen later took one brief trip back to Penn State to make arrange-ments to begin classes again next trimester. Otherwise, she remained with her brother. She brought him books. She spent hours talking to him and rubbing his back and hands. The two had always had a bond, ever since Hugh's earliest years, when Ellen had watched over him. They were alike, too. Ellen had always been obsessive, about school and studying, for example. They expected the same thing of themselves: perfection.

———————— • ————————

One day a man with black hair and white skin arrived. Dressed in a black coat and stovepipe hat, he looked as if he'd stepped out of Oliver Twist's London. He asked Hugh whether he might come in, talk to him, and pray with him. "Our whole church is praying for you," he said. His name was Jerry White, and he was a chimney sweep and a pastor.

Had Hugh's parents been there, they probably wouldn't have let him in. So many people and reporters had been through that the par-ents had finally told the front desk, "Please, no one else." But Hugh liked this man's manner and said yes.

The chimney sweep stayed an hour that first day, and after that came four or five more times, staying over an hour each visit. Sometimes he brought his wife. He held Hugh's and Jeff's hands as he prayed. Hugh came to like and respect him. Later the boys could not remember a word the man said, only that his tone had been tremendously loving and encouraging.

"He gives so much," Hugh said to Jeff. "He concentrates so hard when he prays." Another local pastor visited as well. He put a kindly arm about the boys' shoulders, always asking how they were doing.

Steve Grossman, Hugh's friend from Yosemite, phoned. "I was blown away by the news," he said. Then he told Hugh all about the *Jolly Roger*, a new route he and his friend Charles Cole had pioneered on El Capitan. He gave Hugh detailed descriptions of almost every pitch.

Hugh listened with interest. "It sounds almost as classic as *The Nose*," he said, referring to El Cap's best-known route.

———— • ————

Martha Herr wrote to the Dows, trying to express her sorrow over the loss of their son. She received an emotional letter in return.

"We know you are having to be strong too for your young men," it began. "We wish them the best possible and remain anxious as each news bit comes in.

"May we all meet sometime with our strength restored and your boys working on their future. We know they have suffered and we truly wish them the best.

"Marjorie and Albert Dow, Jr."

Meeting in a special session, the state senate quickly passed a bill providing volunteers on rescue teams the same workers' compensation offered to state employees. Two weeks after the accident, on March 18, Governor Hugh Gallen signed Senate Bill 22, as several members of the North Conway rescue team stood by him. A supplementary budget included eighty thousand dollars for new radio and other equipment.

In the events leading up to that legislation John Herr found an explanation for some of the public criticism. Fish and Game, having lost funding the previous autumn, had used the events of the rescue to lobby for more. The situation lent itself to being held up as validation: Fish and Game was overworked and underfunded, the rescuers had done a superb job, the boys were alive. John Herr surmised that it was in hopes of receiving aid that the Fish and Game director had made his hard-line comments.

"It's politics, Hugh," he told his son.

Hugh turned that over in his mind. Then he heard, during a conversation with a friend who'd heard it somewhere else, that Henry Barber, always his idol, had said, "Those stupid kids."

———— • ————

Hugh never felt more helpless and dependent than when he was with his nurses. Nor did he feel the community sentiment more acutely through anyone else.

There were no overtly hostile words. It was mostly just the feeling he got when, for example, a nurse was supposed to change his bandages and didn't, or when a nurse snapped at him when he asked for a drink of water.

"I can't complain," he thought. "People have a right to be pissed."

All he wanted was to get out of New Hampshire.

Through Hugh's remorse and anger emerged purpose. Out of respect for Albert, no matter what happened, he could not pity himself and give up. "Not to try," he reasoned, "would be a degradation to myself and to Albert's memory."

10

On February 11, sixteen days after his rescue, Hugh was taken to the airport. He was to be transferred by small plane to the Presbyterian Medical Center at the University Hospital in Philadelphia, an hour and a half away from his home in Lancaster. Circulation to his feet remained poor, and tissue necrosis evidenced infection.

Hugh was wheeled to the ambulance in blowing snow. It was the first time he had been outdoors since the rescue. A New Hampshire doctor was saying good-bye, but it was all Hugh could do to answer: the snow had sent him into a near-panic. It made him think of lying under a rock, of dying on a mountainside, of run-stepping downhill toward treeline. He was overwhelmed by a sick feeling of terrible uncertainty, then feverishly imagined he was dying. "But I'm alive," he told himself confusedly.

His doctor had taken Ellen aside. "I'm worried," he told her. "I feel like your family is getting its hopes up. His feet are getting worse every day. I'm afraid he'll lose them."

Hugh slept a little on the nearly three-hour plane trip but then woke, nauseated, trying not to vomit. He was running a high fever, and it hurt to move. He lay as still as possible.

When the plane touched down in spring weather in Philadelphia, Hugh looked out and saw a television crew waiting on the pavement. His parents had intended the trip to be quiet, but somehow word had leaked out.

As he was lifted onto a gurney, Martha Herr tried to answer the questions the reporters were asking. "Mother," Ellen said sharply, grabbing her arm. "Come *on*. Huey's sick. We can talk later." Hugh hid his face with his hands, feeling like a criminal.

Ellen watched as Dr. Frederick Reichle, a vascular surgeon at Presbyterian, unwrapped the bandages. From across the room, she could see only raw, red patches on skinny calves, and dark blue and black skin. Earlier the discoloration and swelling had been confined to Hugh's feet. She was discouraged by the disturbed looks on the doctors' faces.

"His is the worst case of frostbite I've seen in twenty years," Reichle told reporters afterward. "The chances of saving his feet are guarded." Privately, he told the Herr parents that the chances of saving them were slim; he did not bring up the subject with Hugh.

Reichle wanted to begin an experimental surgical process in which Hugh's arteries would be parted; he would treat Hugh at no cost. Nevertheless, and despite insurance, the Herrs' medical bills would eventually approach a hundred thousand dollars. The hospital offered some services without charge, such as allowing Martha and Ellen to move into a suite adjacent to Hugh's room.

Though he never said so, his mother and sister both sensed that Hugh dreaded going to bed at night. It was nearly impossible for him to sleep because of the pain. Nights were long ordeals.

The third night he was at Presbyterian he woke in horror to the sounds of screams coming down the hall from other patients. He lay rigid, a film of sweat covering him quickly like a clammy plastic wrap. It was not the last time he would hear screams. "This place is like a torture chamber," he thought.

His father came to the hospital several times a week. One day Hugh asked him, "Dad, will I be able to climb again?"

"If you want to climb, you'll climb again, with or without feet," John Herr said. "Right now you don't even need to think about it. You have a lot of other things to think about. You need to get strong first."

———— • ————

Hugh underwent an arteriogram, an x-ray of the arteries after they have been injected with radio-opaque dye. The procedure was to test the function of his arteries, to check for narrowing and occlusions, to see what was working and what was not.

A nurse arrived in the morning and swabbed him clean above each thigh, between hip and groin. He was given no premedication; he was already on a large amount of morphine. Then he was placed on a gurney and wheeled to the x-ray department. In x-ray, the cart turned right, then stopped.

An x-ray machine was strapped to the ceiling, affixed to a rack so that it could slide back and forth. A technician positioned it just above Hugh. A doctor took a tube from an infuser, a machine like a large syringe, at Hugh's side and attached a Y-adapter to the tube's end. Everyone wore white coats. Hugh was stiff with dread, surrounded by equipment, his arms held out at his sides by metal straps.

"Hugh," said one doctor, "we're going to place a needle in each of your femoral arteries, and then slowly infuse some dye into them. You may feel a great deal of pressure, but it will last only about half a minute."

Hugh was thinking to himself, "You know when a doctor tells you that, it's really gonna be outrageous."

The doctors, technician, and nurse stepped out of the room. Their faces reappeared on the other side of a window, peering at him. They also looked at a series of gauges, including a monitor that would show the flow of dye in his arteries.

Hugh waited, alert, feeling like a captive animal in a mad scientist's experiment. Since being hospitalized, he had developed a way of psyching himself up for pain by relaxing. He willfully relaxed now and consciously did not anticipate the moment the pain would hit. He knew that if he could take the blow when he was calm, it would be ten times easier, physically and psychologically.

At the same time he also concentrated on what he was feeling, rather than trying to ignore it. He remembered, long before, reducing something advanced and complex to an essence. As a middle-schooler, he had run track. At one point he had said to himself, casting off thoughts of timing and starts and strategies, "All I have to do is move my legs fast."

Now he thought, "It's just another feeling."

The machine above him emitted a series of clicks and beeps, and a warm, stinging sensation gave him time to think only that this was it before it reached a fast, terrible crescendo. He thought his legs would explode, that parts of them would fly all over the room, like something in a horror movie. The intensity of his scream increased with the pressure.

Afterward, a technician came back into the room and lifted the x-ray machine away. His tones were businesslike. "Well, you survived it," he said.

Back in his room Hugh sobbed and sobbed. All he could say to his mother was, "It was horrible."

A few days later began a string of seven surgeries over three weeks, during which Hugh was frequently kept in the intensive care unit overnight. He hardly ever slept when he was there, and when he did, he had nightmares. He didn't tell his mother; she heard it from a nurse.

The morphine made Hugh feel positive. He built up hope that things would be different. That thought gave him relief.

He was to be on morphine for a month without realizing that he was becoming addicted. All he knew was that the morphine delivered him from pain. And it was the only way he could sleep.

———— • ————

Hugh began asking his mother, "Where's Tony? Why isn't he coming?"

Martha Herr knew why Tony, whose presence and approval had always been so important to Hugh, was procrastinating. Her mild, serene oldest child had a way of avoiding trauma and emotion. He tended to be very deeply affected and thought he couldn't cope.

She called Tony's wife, Sally, and said, "Get him down here."

Two weeks after Hugh's arrival in Philadelphia, Tony appeared at the hospital. He was defensive, sheepish, numb, filled with denial and touched with anger and exasperation. He felt a profound sadness he could not articulate or compartmentalize, and he seemed to have nowhere to put it. He wondered what he would say. He couldn't tell his brother, "I understand"–because he didn't. Nothing awful had ever happened to Tony.

He and Sally met Martha in the hall outside Hugh's room. "Don't leave me," he said to them. They walked toward the door, but as he entered the room, the two women dropped back and disappeared.

Across the room, Hugh, propped up on pillows and with a TV murmuring, raised his head. Tony barely noticed his thinness and pallor; he was struck by the sheen of sweat all over his brother's body. "He looks strung out," Tony thought. "God, he looks like a junkie."

"How are you?" asked Tony. "How do you feel?" He sat beside the bed, his lean limbs aligned in his habitual, almost feminine grace. He glanced around. The walls were covered with cards, and the room was full of gifts: paintings, drawings, books, fruit, chocolates, large unopened envelopes full of still more mail.

"O.K.," said Hugh. In his voice was no reproach that Tony had taken so long to come, nothing but a reply.

"Sorry I didn't get here sooner," said Tony.

"That's O.K.," said Hugh. His lip quivered. "Tony," he said urgently, "what about climbing?"

Tony leaned forward. "Don't worry," he began.

He was about to say more when Hugh blurted out, "I'm sorry, Tony." He started to cry. He needed to be forgiven and to hear from Tony that things were going to be all right.

Tony jumped onto the edge of the bed and pulled his brother into his arms. "It's O.K.," he said. "It's O.K., man."

They held each other a long time before Tony spoke again. "Even if the worst happens, if you really want to, you're going to climb. Everything's gonna be O.K."

In the hospital reception area, Tony saw his father. He approached, not knowing what to say.

"The only thing that kid cares about is whether he'll climb again, and if girls'll go for him," John said. "Can you believe that?" They both laughed, and the tension was broken.

John seemed fascinated by his youngest son's single-mindedness. Tony realized that his father finally understood how deeply the boys cared about climbing, and how much it was, for Hugh, an obsession.

———————— • ————————

Jeff Batzer was at Lancaster General Hospital. Circulation to his right hand and left foot was poor; both extremities were infected.

On March 2, Jeff's doctor amputated the young man's right thumb and four fingers down to the first joint. Three days later he amputated Jeff's left foot and the toes of his right foot.

———————— • ————————

At Presbyterian, Hugh was unsettled and irritable, physically drained by gangrene. His feet turned black; they looked mummified, shrunken, and dead. In New Hampshire he had been able to move them, but now he could not.

He was undergoing debridement, surgery to clean his deteriorating flesh and scrape dead tissue from the surface, up to twice a week; he was having general anesthesia again and again. It was increasingly difficult to swim back up from each such dream-and-pain period. No sooner would he feel conscious and lucid than it would be time for the next surgery. In one way, though, he always displayed the resilience of a kid: after each operation, he could eat right away.

He received so many needles—morphine injections, antibiotic shots, and IVs—that one day his veins collapsed. Nurse after nurse came in and tried to insert another IV. An intern tried, the fourth person, and finally got the needle into the vein. Once Hugh got a morphine shot in the backside, and the needle hit his bone.

Through the thin hospital walls he heard more screams in the night. His conversation these days was minimal, practical: about getting shots on time, or plans for the next surgery.

Mostly, he looked forward to being home, not in terms of doing or seeing specific things, or of certain memories, but just to being there.

———————— • ————————

Over and over Hugh asked his doctors and nurses whether they could save his feet. Sometimes they said kindly maybes; sometimes they said they didn't know, but that he would walk again.

Jeff had said resignedly, of his frostbitten extremities, "Get rid of them." But Hugh was more persistent and stubborn. It was becoming clear to him that his feet were gone, but he wouldn't admit it.

They didn't look like feet. In New Hampshire they had been swollen like balloons, but now they were shrunken. All the tissue around one ankle had either rotted or been cleaned away, and his bone showed through, an inch and a half, yellow-brown. Scaly black skin stretched around the edges of the bone and curled back to show the red inner layers. Across the feet, the skin bore no resemblance to skin. What wasn't black was purple, red, or yellow, the flesh soft, folded, and draped. The toes were pitch black, and most of them had fused and bonded together.

The first time Hans saw his brother's feet, as he stood in the room while a nurse changed the bandages, his vision went black. He backed up involuntarily and sat down, taking deep breaths to control his dizziness. Until that moment he had wanted to believe what the doctors had said, that Hugh might keep his legs.

Hugh glanced at Hans and then looked down at his mutilated feet. Whenever anyone changed his bandages, Hugh watched. He never touched his feet, but he always looked. He could smell them, a sharp, nauseating odor. He kept trying to think what it reminded him of, and one day it came to him. They smelled just like an animal killed on the road, when you drive by a day or two afterward.

On top of that were the odors of medicine, chemicals, and himself. He was given sponge baths, but they couldn't take away the rankness.

Hugh had physical therapy daily. A nurse would take his bandages off and help him place his feet in the current of the whirlpool. The water wasn't bubbly but clear, and he could see the ragged shreds of skin wave back and forth. Scraps of skin always floated to the top.

Seeing Hugh staring at his feet, Ellen finally lost her composure. "Why do you keep looking at them?" she said. "Please don't look at them!" She turned and staggered out.

Hugh sat alone. "I wish I could run, too," he thought. "But I can't get away from it."

He thought that she had left because she was sickened by the sight. But she left because she felt he was being tortured. She wanted the feet gone. There was so little tissue left that she could see through them to the bottom of the whirlpool. She had been thinking, "Hugh, don't look, don't hurt yourself any more."

He'll lose his feet and he'll never climb again, she reasoned. She'd just read a letter to Hugh from an Australian who'd lost both legs in a train crash. That man couldn't walk. And here Hugh was talking about climbing. "He's dreaming," she thought.

One morning shortly afterward, Martha woke Ellen. It was early: the suite was gray, the shades pulled. "Come quick," she said. "Dr. Reichle's going to tell Huey he has to have his amputations tomorrow."

Reichle was sitting down beside Hugh. He placed his clipboard on his lap. "Hugh," he said gently, "we've decided to amputate."

Hugh's eyes watered. "But I can feel things down there," he said.

"We can wait a week."

Hugh was silent for a moment. Then he said, "Let's do it."

Ellen watched. Reichle left. Hugh didn't seem to react.

Later that day, Hugh asked his nurse, "Will this be more painful than what I've already gone through?"

"It will probably be twice as painful, at least," she said.

Hugh said faintly, "Really?"

"Yes, it's going to be extremely painful."

Ellen was shaking her head, thinking, "Please don't tell him that now. Please."

That night she came into his room. She often talked to him and gave him backrubs at night, when his pain increased. Now she slipped a Police tape into the cassette deck and began massaging his back.

He spoke into the pillow, saying something about his feet. "Maybe they should wait," he said, his voice indistinct.

"Oh, Huey, you're much better off this way," Ellen said. "This is going on too long. You're just getting sicker. You're not losing your feet tomorrow, Huey. You already lost them. You left them in the woods in New Hampshire. You know that, don't you?"

That was when he let loose, and cried and cried.

Later, before he slept, he told his mother, "I don't want 'em anymore. They're so useless."

He remembered something from another world, a long time ago, that his worst fear was of becoming physically handicapped–losing his athleticism, and losing the acceptance of his peers.

Ellen left the next morning, when Hugh was being wheeled into surgery. She couldn't take any more–she didn't know whether she could stand what he would go through after the operation–and she knew her father would be there with her mother. She hugged a nurse who had been friendly to her. "Please, please take care of my little brother," she said.

———— • ————

When Hugh began to surface from the anesthesia, he screamed. He was incoherent. His parents stood beside the bed, holding hands and praying.

But Hugh didn't remember that part. His memory was of waking alone. He knew right away where he was and what had happened. The first thing he saw was the smooth sheets below his knees. He shoved the covers aside and looked at his legs. He was horrified to see how short they were. He had thought he would lose the unhealthy section below his boot top.

In surgery, Reichle had removed both of Hugh's legs four and a half inches below the knee, leaving part of each calf on the back of the leg to wrap over the wound. Four inches below the knee is considered the standard amputation length, the right length for plugging a limb end into a prosthesis.

But Hugh was livid, thinking there had been an injustice, a terrible mistake. "They should be longer!" he said to himself in consternation. He began crying, talking out loud. "I can't believe they did this!"

———— • ————

John Herr came in and looked down on Hugh. "Well, you're handicapped now," he said softly. Hugh ducked his head. "You don't like the sound of that, do you?"

"No," Hugh said.

"Good. I hope you never like the sound of that. You're going to do just fine, Hugh."

He handed Hugh a book, *The Love of Mountains*, by Michael Crawford Poole. John had written on the flyleaf,

Dear Hugh,

Remember the beauty, the mistakes, the zeal, the cold, the friends, the stupidity, the guts, the pain, the warmth, the anguish, the despair, the triumph, the love, and the almighty and merciful God in Heaven—in the young winter of 1982.

Mother and Dad

In the days that followed, phantom pains—sensations that in a cruel irony seem to be located in an absent limb—set in. They were unpredictable, veering from dull to sudden, sharp, and piercing. Soon they were chronic.

Hugh was being given morphine every three hours. Exactly an hour and a half after each dose, he would sit up and say, "What time is it?" His father or mother would reply. Then he would rock, his eyes closed and his muscles tense, waiting.

One of his best moments came when, for the first time since the accident, Hugh got out of bed. He marveled to be sitting in a chair, and on a different side of the room.

Then, three days after the surgery, his morphine dosage was abruptly reduced. He was taken from a shot every three hours to one a day.

The shock was enormous. Except for the one hour a day following his injection, Hugh sat hunched, or fidgeted, thrashed, and pleaded. He called the nurses over and over on the intercom, begging, "Please give me a shot."

That was the only time his mother left, unable to bear seeing her son in this state. Her husband told her, "I'm staying, you're going."

"I can't drive out of Philadelphia, I don't know the way," she said helplessly, feeling as if she could cope with nothing.

"It's easy." He began giving the directions.

"The heck with it," she said, interrupting him. "I'm going."

In the car she put a tape of soothing classical music into the cassette player. She got herself out of the city and then cried the whole way home, giving vent to two months' worth of emotion and tension. She hadn't cried since the night Hugh was found.

Relieved and unloaded, she wandered around the farmhouse, wanting to do manual, mundane things. The house was clean, but the quilt she had been making when Hugh was lost was still waiting in its frame. She lifted it out and put the frame away. She wouldn't finish it this winter, and so it might as well be out of the way.

She wanted to cook. She tried to think of things Hugh might like to eat and decided on a blueberry pie. Standing in her sunny kitchen, mixing and rolling the pale dough, she found peace again. Flattening the crust, placing it in the pan, and crimping its edges all had a therapeutic, sedative normalcy. The next day, she went back to the hospital with a fresh pie in her hands.

By now Martha had lost twenty pounds, and her hair had become as stiff and hard as straw. She went to a hairdresser and asked, "What's wrong with my hair? It's like a fright wig." She thought it might have gotten that way from chlorine or hospital soap. It had also become much grayer than before.

"That's what happens when you go through stress," the hairdresser said. "I've seen it before. It'll tame down after a while."

———— • ————

Four days after the surgery, Nancy Aument, the twenty-four-year-old daughter of family friends, walked into Hugh's room for a surprise visit. Hugh looked over at her, but her eyes had fallen on the empty spaces in his sheets. She gasped and ran out of the room. She hadn't known about the amputations. Her mother called Martha later to apologize.

Five days after the surgery, a nurse told Hugh, "I can give you some pills for the pain."

"Forget it," Hugh said. "They won't even affect me." The nurse didn't argue.

Hugh was seeking to exercise some control. He was fighting for a bit of his old purist ethic—no drugs, no pills, keep the body clean.

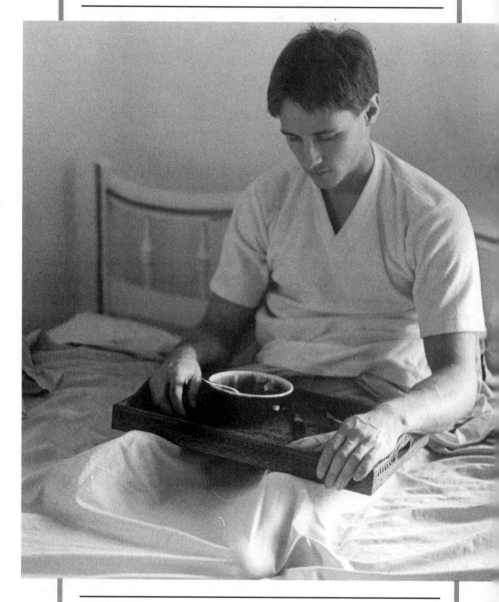

HH

The morphine-withdrawal symptoms had overwhelmed him. He felt pain and some nausea, but almost worse was a pervasive hollowness, as if he had no soul. There was no way he could read, or even watch a movie on TV. He could register nothing that wasn't completely mindless. All he could do was watch cartoons. He watched silently. He sometimes smiled.

———— • ————

His friends and teachers called and wrote. One day his entire gymnastics team came to see him. He dreaded the visit and even tried to back out of it, telling his mother that he was feeling down and didn't want to see them. "Come on, Hugh," she said, "they've come all the way here."

He asked her to help him arrange the covers thickly around his stumps, to fill the spaces. She stuffed a blanket under his sheet and plumped the bedspread over them.

Martha met the ten students in the hallway, before they reached his room. They were as nervous as Hugh. When they asked Martha what to expect, she realized they were concerned about his condition, embarrassed more for his sake than for their own.

"It's O.K.," she said. "Don't worry. You won't notice any difference. He looks the same as he always looked."

"Would you please go in with us?" one student asked. She paused, and said yes.

They first thing they noticed was the strong smell of antiseptic, then the thinness of Hugh's face. He, who had always exuded physical strength, looked white and sick and weak. An intravenous needle was taped into his arm.

The students jumbled shyly around the bed. "Hey, Hugh-Dad," someone said, using an old team nickname.

Others took it up. "Hugh-Dad!" the voices said in hearty tones.

Hugh said a quiet, embarrassed "Hi," his eyes darting. He saw Diane, who had been his girlfriend at the time of the accident. She had called and written several times since, persisting even though his responses had been discouraging. Now she came and stood by his bed, looming awkwardly close, placing her hands in a series of tentative poses and places: pockets, bedpost, folded beneath her elbows. The other students fell into a semicircle around the bed.

"We brought you something," said a boy.

"Look."

"We all went to this meet in Hershey."

A framed, autographed photo of the gymnastics champion Kurt Thomas landed in Hugh's hands.

"Thanks."

There was a silence. Martha prompted, "How is gymnastics going?"

"Fine, fine."

Someone offered, "The districts were last weekend."

"At Shippensburg," said another. Shippensburg University had hosted the various county high school teams.

"Are the states next weekend?" asked Martha. She knew that the team must have qualified for the state championships—it always did.

"Yes. Next weekend."

In the next silence, Hugh turned to Bob Mullins. He hadn't known Bob well—Bob was a year ahead of him, a senior—but he had received a compassionate letter from him. He knew Bob felt for him.

"How'd you do?"

"I got some medals," said Bob, smiling a little sheepishly. "In the pommel horse and parallel bars. Third in both."

Then they were both thinking the same thing. Before the accident, Hugh had been getting good on the parallel bars. He was better than Bob on them. At the very least, Hugh would have won a medal at the districts; he might even have been a contender for first place.

Hugh had been able to spring easily from a "peach basket"—grasping the bars from a stance, then swinging his legs above him and releasing his hands from underneath the bar to grab it from above—up into a handstand. He could also start sideways on one bar and go into a glide kip, swinging his body straight back until he was facing down, parallel to the bars, then swooshing below the bars, jackknifing to point his toes above his head, and thrusting his legs up. He had been working on pressing an English handstand, from a straddle L with one hand in front of the other on a single bar, but he hadn't thrown that in competition yet.

112

Referring to the upcoming state championships, Hugh said, "Kick Chris Reigel's butt." Everyone laughed. That had sounded right, anyway.

Chris, sixteen, had made the Junior Olympics team at age twelve and had almost reached the Olympics, finishing the trials tied for twelfth with an Olympian, Tom Beach. Hugh and the others knew of his beautiful parallel bar work and vaulting. His picture had been on the cover of *International Gymnast*. Chris was from their area, but he trained at a private club, the Gymnastrum Sportschool, so of course he was regarded with envy and reverse snobbery, and as a rival.

"How about that guy Charlie from Manheim Township?" someone began.

The others clamorously joined in. "Oh, *Charlie!*" They burst out laughing in a forced bond with the speaker. It seemed many seconds later that they turned to Hugh and explained how Charlie had been flustered at gymnastics meets.

Hugh nodded. It seemed too late for him to laugh.

"So . . . how's the food?"

"I hate it," said Hugh. He knew he sounded sullen.

They stayed for half an hour. Hugh remained withdrawn, his responses short.

Diane lingered longest. Then she left, too. "Good-bye," she said, peering at him. "Good-bye. Well . . . see you."

———— • ————

Ten days after the surgery Hugh felt much better. The amputations had cleared the gangrene from his system. His energy came back. So did his spirit.

Bob Mullins came to visit again. He had just been to a college interview in Philadelphia, and though it was after visiting hours, the hospital staff allowed him and his mother to come in.

Bob had recently sent Hugh a package of food: nuts, crackers, cereal, and dried fruit. He'd sent some rock-and-roll tapes, too.

"The change," Bob said to Hugh, "is amazing." Hugh looked better, had regained some color. He even joked a bit.

Diane had finally stopped phoning. Hugh never told her to, but he essentially ignored her until she gave up. He had the impression that she very much wanted to continue the relationship. That had surprised him. He hadn't thought she would be able to deal with the situation, but it pleased him that she wanted to.

Still, he needed time to be alone. He was longing for female companionship, but he was self-conscious about his legs. He was haunted by the question of how girls would look at him now. Would they think he was a freak?

One nurse, Julie, who came on duty at three in the afternoons, was friendly. Hugh and the morning-shift nurse had dropped to strictly professional exchanges. But this one was more lighthearted and frank. She was pretty, too—slim, with long brown hair. For days now Hugh had tried to summon up the nerve to ask her whether she could ever be attracted to a man with no legs. He never did, though.

Because Hugh spoke so little, his doctors and nurses thought he was deeply depressed; they sent in clergymen and psychiatrists. But his father told them, "That's just his way. Let him deal with it."

Hugh's family had always been so self-sufficient that the idea of counseling sat ill with them. They did not think therapy would help. "You've had amputees before," John Herr said to Hugh's doctor. "But have you ever had a seventeen-year-old rock climber from Lancaster?"

Hugh dreamed of climbing again. He'd never lost the desire; the question was, could he? He didn't even know whether he would ever walk again.

Outside the hospital, one of the Gunks climbers said, "He'll never climb again. Well, if he does, he'll only climb five-six."

In Arizona, Steve Grossman thought, "His life is shattered. He was so focused. He has nothing left."

Lying in the hospital, Hugh reasoned, "If I can walk, I can climb. Babies pull themselves up on their crib rails before they can walk. I'll have to be like a baby."

He didn't dare predict that he might climb at any high level. He thought about it, though. He thought about it all the time.

Some of what drove him was shame and rage, thoughts that he had failed as a climber and a person. Some of it was that he wanted attention from the world. And he didn't want to lose his friends.

And the rest was that he simply *was* a climber. Climbing was Hugh's identity, his picture of himself, the source of the greatest moments of his life. He remembered the joy he used to feel. It was difficult for him to imagine feeling joy again. It was hard to think of himself throwing his head back and laughing a deep, real laugh.

"You could do other things," Hans said to Hugh. He assumed that the doctor he'd asked was right, and that Hugh probably wouldn't climb again. Nor could Hans imagine how it would be possible. Instead, he wanted to encourage Hugh in a positive direction, to talk about something for which there could be a shred of hope. "You could get into flying."

"Yeah," Hugh said, and began talking about something else.

Hans waited. "There's a paraplegic pilot," he said. "Chris Starbuck. People launch him. He's flown sixty miles, from Mahatango, this mountain in Appalachia, to Downington. That's where he's from. He flew home."

Hugh just said, "Yeah," and changed the subject again.

Hans thought, "I guess you won't go down without trying." He understood. Even though he virtually never climbed anymore, he thought, "I wouldn't want to say I *don't* climb." Climbing was too much a part of the Herr brothers, and they were too much a part of its world, the subculture of its community.

Recovering now, after the surgery, Hugh practiced his craft. He eased out of bed, slid on the floor to the window, and lifted and moved his weight from side to side on the window ledge. In bed he worked on one-arm pull-ups, clutching the metal triangle used for maneuvering in and out of bed.

Morris Hershoff phoned from New York. He asked Hugh how he was and chatted a little. "Some of the guys here want to come down and see you," he said.

"Thanks," Hugh said, "but forget it, just wait a while. Then we'll get together, O.K.?"

Hugh's relationship with the Gunks climbers was, essentially, about climbing. To him, having them visit now would be depressing. "I want to have them see me climbing," he thought, "looking good."

The volume of mail increased. One letter was from President Reagan. "I think you are a young man with a very brave heart," it read. A letter came from Alaska, from a man who described himself as "a gay male in my fifties . . . with a recently acquired interest in amputees."

Hugh wished another amputee, especially an active one, would visit him in the hospital. He received a few letters from amputees, but they were sedentary people. One girl wrote that she walked and used her wheelchair only sometimes, and he thought, "Oh, shit."

But soon afterward, his physical therapist, Frank Malone, reassured him that he would be able to do ninety percent of what he had always done.

"You'll never be able to run," said Malone gently. "If you can climb at all, it will be limited. What else do you like to do? Ski? You'll be able to do that."

"I don't want to," said Hugh. "Nothing to do with snow."

11

About two weeks after the amputations, Hugh went home for three weeks. His parents drove him from the hospital and wheeled him to the back door. Outside the fields were greening in the warm weather, and there were weeds in the yard. Inside, his family, a few close friends, and their children all stood calling choruses of hellos. A big sign read, "Welcome home, Hugh." Balloons and streamers hung from the ceiling, and a cake and rows of paper cups waited on the table. Heidi, the family's German shepherd, was the first to run up and greet him.

Hugh, beaming sheepishly, thought, "I am finally really home."

That night he had a vivid dream, based on a scene from J.R.R. Tolkien's *The Hobbit*. The hobbit Bilbo and his dwarf friends are lost in Mirkwood, a black forest. Drafted for the job because he is the lightest, Bilbo climbs a tall tree to see whether he can determine their location. When his head breaks through the top branches, for the first time in days he feels the wind on his face. Transfixed by the wind and sun, he barely hears the impatient questions from below.

In Hugh's dream, he felt fresh air moving and stirring across his face, just like Bilbo's. But the sensation wasn't due to blowing wind;

rather, Hugh was doing the one thing that, during waking hours, he knew he would probably never do: running. He had legs.

When he woke, he was sad but thankful for the release. Hugh liked the dream. It came to him for two months. He rarely missed a night.

———————— • ————————

The next morning, the first thing Hugh did was scuttle into the kitchen, scooting on his backside, legs extended forward. He pulled himself up onto a chair and then manteled onto the counter. Reaching up, he folded his hands over the top of the refrigerator, fingers stretched out flat, thumbs bent across the first joints of his forefingers. With a little "hu-uh" of breath, he swung himself around the front of the refrigerator, then past its doors to the other side. He dropped down onto straight arms and leaned his head back. It was heavenly to stretch out his back. Then he did ten pull-ups on the refrigerator.

He palmed his way back around to the counter and sat there panting, dreamy. It was the first time since his accident that he had been in a fully upright position.

Then he moved along the floor to the basement door. Carefully, holding on to the rail, he inched himself down the stairs, and then behind them. He put his hands on the rung just above his head, weighted them, lifted his hips an inch, and then reached for the next rung. Swinging hand over hand, he climbed up the underside of the basement stairs, legs flying free above the concrete floor. He felt weak and thought of stopping when he got two thirds of the way up, but the motions felt so good that he kept going. He made it all the way to the top but then could barely get down, hands slapping madly.

On the floor, he felt dizzy and his ears were blocked from the physical stress, but he smiled. When he thought of his frantic motions to get down, he laughed out loud.

———————— • ————————

Hugh was happy to be home but overwhelmed. He had a sense of just wanting to be alone and sit and not have anything come toward him. He sometimes yearned to stay in his house always, safe and buffered, and never go anywhere.

He did, however, like to have Bob Mullins come over. The two of them often sat in the family room and watched TV for hours, never saying a word. Hugh's mother wondered whether Hugh shouldn't be making an effort to entertain Bob. But the two youths made a connection that was stronger for being wordless. It had always been a labor for Hugh to hold a conversation. Bob, a particularly intelligent, sensitive boy, had never found social interaction easy, either.

They took up backgammon and played it often. They played some chess. Martha Herr always seemed to have a pot of something – chili or spaghetti (eating that with peanut butter was a favorite Herr family tradition) – around for them. They never did speak of the accident, but Hugh sometimes told Bob what he was feeling physically. Of the phantom sensations, he said once, "A lot of times my feet *itch*. But there aren't any feet there to scratch." Other times it seemed as though his missing feet hurt: the pains would come with no warning. For a few seconds they would be very sharp, then they would stop. It felt as if someone were stabbing his feet with a handful of needles, then pulling them out. Sometimes, during the first months, as he extended a leg toward a hot tub, he could feel his invisible foot touch the water first.

The letters and phone calls about the accident still came to Lancaster. Some were harsh; a few were from local newspapers, wanting Hugh's opinion on the controversy ongoing in the New Hampshire press.

———— • ————

After Hugh's visit at home, he spent three weeks at the McGee Rehabilitation Center in Philadelphia. His parents took him there and wheeled his chair into the large, square, brick building.

A nurse steered Hugh past green lobby plants and down long corridors to show him around. As they entered the large common room, with its television, pool table, magazines, Coke machine, and the metallic bars, wheels, and boxes of equipment, his gaze landed on a quadraplegic. A nurse was holding a cigarette to the man's mouth. She lowered it as he exhaled, waited, and raised it again.

Hugh, mesmerized, suddenly felt lucky for the first time since the accident. He looked around and saw people who were deformed, maimed, immobile, their pale faces peering above neck braces and twisted torsos.

Several people wore external fixation devices – halos – around their necks to stabilize fractures. Some, with broken backs, wore turtle-shell braces, rigid shields that encased their torsos. They were in wheel-chairs. Others had respirators over their noses and mouths, and some-one was hooked to a suction machine; a nurse held a tube in his mouth to remove the excretion.

An electric wheelchair coming from the opposite direction passed Hugh as he was wheeled to his room. The center had put all of the five male amputees together. Three were in their seventies, and two of them appeared to be senile. Hugh could see that because of his youth and health, and the extent of his injuries, he was the best off among them. He had his hands and his knees.

"Hi there, 'uey!" said the fourth man, thrusting his arm straight out to shake hands. He seemed to be about forty. "I'm Tony." Hugh thought the way Tony pronounced his name was funny.

The room contained six beds, three to a side. After stowing his things in a dresser, Hugh's parents lingered. When they eventually left, Hugh felt uneasy in his new situation. But mostly he was eager to get started, to get through rehab, to get his artificial legs.

That night he chatted for a few minutes with Tony, who told Hugh all about his family, his home in New York, his ex-wife. He was lively and animated. Hugh could see that Tony would be the only one in the room he could talk to, but also that this good-natured, garrulous person would be incapable of giving advice, on rehabilitation or life.

Before he went to sleep, he lay on his bed, trying to read. He felt as if he had been slapped in the face. This was a different reality, nothing to do with his world of farms, mountains, and athleticism.

At about ten-fifteen the telephone by his bed rang. "Hey, Hugh, how you doin'?" It was the voice of Russ Raffa, calling from New Paltz. Hugh hardly knew him but had seen him around. Russ was good-looking, glib, and animated. He was older than Hugh, and known as one of the Gunks' leading climbers.

They chatted a minute or two. "So when are you going to be climb-ing again?" Raffa asked casually.

Hugh couldn't believe his ears. Blood rushed up into his face and prickled in his scalp. No one had come out and asked him about climbing.

"Yes, I want to."

"Well, you haven't missed anything," said Raffa, his conversational tone unchanged. "The weather's been lousy. It's been raining a lot."

The next day Hugh was racing up and down the hall in his wheelchair, speeding around the corners. He'd adjusted so quickly that it seemed as if he'd been at McGee for months.

Hugh's first pair of legs were made of plaster of paris and called pylons. They had plaster sockets and would be attached with straps above the knee. He was turning them over in his hands when the prosthetist brought out a box of feet. Hugh begged him to find a pair that his climbing shoes would fit over. "Look, they need to be narrow, and about this long."

Smiling, the prosthetist put down the foot he was holding. "Relax, Hugh," he said.

Later that day Hugh visited his doctor. "What will I be able to do?" he asked.

"Well, Hugh, you might eventually be able to walk without canes, and you probably can ride a bike, and you could drive a car with hand controls, but you'll never be able to climb those mountains again."

Hugh froze. His thoughts rattled. "This guy knows what he's talking about, and he's telling me I won't be able to do much."

On the first day Hugh was to try walking, his therapist accompanied him as he rolled his wheelchair to the end of a set of parallel bars and parked it. Hugh thought, "*This* is gonna hurt."

He fitted his leg ends in the sockets of the pylons, clutched the bars, and stood up. He gasped and sat right back down again, even though he had not weighted his legs fully. He wanted to scream. Pain pierced his stumps, whose stitches had only recently been removed.

"I can't imagine this ever working," he thought.

One day during the first week, Hugh bouldered a little on the wall of the therapy room, legs dragging. His doctor caught him and told him to get down. The doctor thought he was crazy.

One of Hugh's physicians was Carolyn Kinney, a twenty-four-year-

LANCASTER COUNTY, PENNSYLVANIA   HH

old resident in rehabilitative medicine. Kinney worked under the supervision of Hugh's attending physician and, in turn, supervised his therapists. After the accounts she'd read and heard, she expected Hugh to be a reckless teenager.

She felt tentative, not knowing what her young patient's emotional state might be, both because of the loss of his feet and because he was seeing so many profoundly injured people. She began asking him questions. He didn't offer much, but he answered every question, and so she kept on.

"We made some mistakes," he told her. She asked him to describe the accident and felt he had accepted responsibility for his role. She told her boyfriend, Will Eckhardt, a climber, that Hugh showed depth and understanding about the decisions.

"When I realized that he wasn't a jerk, I really empathized with him, and I'm really interested in his case," she said. "He's not an irresponsible person. I think he's pretty mature. He seems older than seventeen."

She noticed that Hugh didn't mix with the other patients. In the gym she usually saw him by himself, working on his walking. He talked mostly with his therapists. She found it difficult to place him in the same context as the others.

"He's going to go on," she told Eckhardt. "There is a future for him. He's going to be walking well. He's not giving up or changing his life's plans. He's going to get through it."

The first day Hugh went into an exercise class, he grabbed a pair of twenty-five-pound dumbbells and started lifting them so energetically that he was almost throwing them.

"I knew I was in trouble as soon as I saw that," his exercise teacher later teased him.

He was now walking on prostheses, using canes. The act of walking was easy, but the pain was excruciating.

———— • ————

Hugh had never felt closer to people than he had to climbers. The support, the trust, and the sharing of power and problem solving created an almost supernatural bonding. He respected climbers, too, because they cared passionately about what they did.

He had always wanted the approval of the climbing community. Now, though he didn't want other climbers to see him yet, it was important that they were there and behind him. It was important that they thought he could climb – and that his father thought so as well.

The first two weekends he went home from the rehabilitation center, his doctors wouldn't let him take his legs. They knew that if they did, he would go climbing.

The third weekend, when he was allowed to take the pylons, he showed off for his family, walking around, even dancing a few steps, giggling. Then he wanted to go climbing.

He and Tony drove down to Safe Harbor, along the shores of the Susquehanna. They parked the car in silence, beside the old railroad tracks. Hugh pushed open the door and stepped onto the gravel. Tony handed Hugh his canes from the back seat, then stepped around to the trunk to hoist both of their packs and the rope.

Hugh looked out at the river, about half a mile wide here. It was brown from spring runoff, its surface rippled. Surrounding the low mounds of tiny rock islands, new spears of rushes and reeds pierced the water.

He and Tony started off along the train tracks. Hugh could step only on the solid wood of the ties, not the gravel, where he might skid. The beams were too far apart for him to step on alternate ties, and so he took tiny, mincing steps.

About a hundred feet along he came to a slab of rock, fringed in straggly bushes, that led up toward the cliff. He paused and looked at it. The wind rustled all around him. To his left, in the lush, sun-dappled woods, sounded a crash as a branch fell to the ground and bounced once in the weeds. Here was his first climb, this mossy, orangey slab webbed with white lichens.

On all fours, he began. A tentative shuffle worked to get his feet higher. He found two rock mounds to use as handholds and brought his feet up again. He grabbed a bush and pulled higher with that. He crawled two steps on his knees and thus passed his first obstacle.

He stood . . . and fell over.

"Here," said Tony. "I'll bring you along the path on piggyback."

About thirty feet farther the way evened a little. Tony set him down and, as he started hobbling, went back for the canes. Hugh studied the rock. Its surface was flecked in orange and silver, banded with quartz, wet and seeping and slimy in the corners and holes.

Tony uncoiled the rope, and the brothers tied into its ends in silence. They had done this route for a warmup probably a dozen times before. It was a sixty-foot 5.9 named *Cherry Hill*. Tony led off, brushing away a spider web; long gray strands stuck in loops on his shirt-sleeve. He pulled up on an overhang by using several big juggy holds in a row, and walked his feet up, tilting his head to see the toeholds beneath the roof. He grabbed a good left hold, raised himself until his left shoulder was next to his hand, and locked into that position to reach with his right for a shallow, pod-shaped fingerhold, and then a deep tight pod in a crack. He went another ten feet and disappeared around an overlap. Then he was up in the trees.

Now the two spoke only their shortened version of the standard belay commands.

"Got me?"

"You're on."

The first thing Hugh noticed as he began moving up the rock— handhold, handhold, place one foot, place the other—was how much easier it was to move vertically than to struggle on the path. He was relieved—not exactly pleased, simply accepting. It was just a fact: he could climb much better than he could walk.

It was curious, to be climbing again. He couldn't really believe what he was doing, but he automatically moved upward. When his artificial feet swung out into the air below the overhang, he clutched two jugs with viselike grips, kicked the feet back in, and planted one on a ledge. He pulled around the roof, sweat glistening on his arms, and hopped his hand upward for the first pod, then upward again for the better one. He barely made it. On the wall above, after three more steps, his lower legs began to slip off. Hanging by one arm, he reached down to hitch them up.

It seemed as if he hadn't hung off his arms for years; he felt huge— heavy and awkward—and thought of the newborn foals he had seen on the farm.

He and Tony drove back to the house, where Hugh's parents and

125

Sally were sitting on the patio, drinking iced tea. Hugh disappeared into the house. He wanted to be alone, to absorb the events and feelings of the last few hours. But he was listening as the sliding door shut behind him.

"Sally, he is incredible," Tony was saying. "Being that weak – and able to climb." Hugh felt good because Tony felt good.

The next day he was climbing the stone foundation in the barn and the cracks in the old corncrib.

"If I had known there was no way to save my feet, I'd have gotten them off right away," he told his mother. "I could have saved myself so much pain, so much misery – gotten an incredible head start. I would have been climbing again so *fast*."

12

As Hugh prepared to leave the rehabilitation center, a Philadelphia news station sought an interview. Hugh balked. John Herr tried to argue with him.

"There has to be some reason for this happening," he said. "Something that people can learn." But the rest of the family backed Hugh, and the father finally gave up.

When Hugh came home, he began playing comic roles. His favorite impression was of television's ferocious Mr. T. "I pity you!" he'd thunder.

Hugh's friend Bob Mullins would tease him back. He'd shake his head and say, "I'm worried about you, Herr."

His family was convulsed with laughter. But when the clowning went on and on, and got to be overdone, his parents knew it was his way of dealing with depression. Hugh had been so serious, so angry, that he needed to balance his emotions by going in the opposite direction.

Neither his parents nor his siblings had ever talked to Hugh about Albert Dow. They hadn't wanted to make him rehash it. The issue had become something they didn't speak of. Now they just let him react in his own way, reasoning that the comedy routines were perhaps a good outlet.

Hugh came up with another mental coping mechanism. The idea always worked best in the morning; he was more vulnerable at night. In the morning, as he sat up and put on his legs, he imagined he was putting on a pair of giant ski boots. He wanted to be normal, to put on normal shoes, and ski boots were more acceptable than medical, clinical, artificial legs. That fantasy took him through his first and second pairs of artificial legs, through the first six months.

———— • ————

With the aid of a tutor, Hugh completed his junior year in high school, but his main focus that spring was bouldering. On a hot, bright day, Hugh's second weekend home from the rehabilitation center, he told Bob Mullins he was taking him to Eshleman Elementary School to learn to climb.

"A school?" Bob asked.

"It's awesome," Hugh assured him. The school's walls were entirely stone.

They arrived in the old olive green Dodge to find the playground full of children, so they moved discreetly to the back of the building. Hugh was still wearing the crude plaster pylons and walking with canes, as the plaster was fragile. He would have to wear the pylons until his stumps had shrunk to a stable size and could be fitted with artificial-leg sockets. The pylons were used to save on expenses; the more advanced artificial legs would cost about $2,000 a pair. Hugh could hardly walk, but he put his EB climbing shoes onto the pylons.

He patiently showed Bob some basics of how to move on rock and then let Bob wear the EBs. Bob wasn't shy about making his first tentative moves on the wall. It was hard to be self-conscious about his own ability, considering what Hugh was working against.

They traded shoes again, and Bob watched Hugh some more, then tried the same moves himself. He was amused that even without natural feet, Hugh was better than he. But Hugh was not pleased.

"This foot doesn't work at all," he said, shaking his head. "It bends easily for walking. But it's hard to stand on a small edge with it."

At the end of an hour Hugh began working at a certain traverse, repeating it several times "for the pump."

"Now," he told Bob, "we do burnouts." They practiced pull-ups on the jungle gym and the overhead ladder until they could do no more. Finally, they did static "hangs," with Hugh insisting they time themselves and try to last certain increments.

"You're a killer, I tell you," said Bob.

One night the two and another friend, Sean, were driving back from climbing at Safe Harbor when Hugh began to moan that he hadn't been keeping his assigned journal for English. His tutor would be asking for it tomorrow.

"Here, we'll help," said Bob. When the three arrived at Hugh's, Bob and Sean wrote several pages in Hugh's notebook. Hugh added some more. It was extremely funny—until the next day, that is, when the tutor noticed three kinds of handwriting.

After two months Hugh received his first pair of sophisticated prosthetic legs. They were made of acrylic resin laminate, and the feet were rubber-coated.

He began experimenting with different kinds of feet for climbing. His first radical design, for cracks, Bob dubbed the Hatchet Foot because from the side, the plastic and rubber creation looked like a blade. As seen from above, it increased in width from its narrow front to the heel. The widening occurred in steps, and each step surface was covered in rubber. Each step could work like a different-sized wedge.

Hugh began to share a few of his tentative design ideas with his climbing friends. One day in late spring Donald Perry called him from the Gunks, greatly excited. "Hugh, we can do it. We can design stuff. I've figured it out. I've got an idea for this leg you can use on *Kansas City*. You'll cruise it!"

———————•———————

As summer arrived, Hugh continued climbing. Practice brought back strength and "feel" as, apart from his phantom pains, Hugh gained a phantom awareness. It seemed that each of his missing feet constantly tingled, the way extremities do after circulation has been cut off and they have gone to sleep. But he was so used to the tingling now that he had to concentrate to feel it.

When he climbed, even when he could not see his feet—when

bulges in the rock hid them—Hugh could tell whether they were on holds. He grew used to the vibrations that traveled through his limb ends. He began to forget how natural feet felt.

Hugh could no longer jump or fall off boulders, as climbers are accustomed to doing. He came to think of bouldering as soloing. Nor could he stand on his toes to reach a high hold.

His dreams about running in the wind continued, but other themes crept in as well. In his chase dreams, Hugh was always ahead of his pursuers. It was not evident how he ran; he just sped along. These chase dreams never had any conclusive ending, and no one ever caught up with him.

He bouldered and practiced walking in intervals of a few days, stopping when he couldn't stand the increasing pain and his mind rebelled against his legs. Then he would take a vacation from them, leaving them off for perhaps three days. Even during comparatively pain-free periods, when Hugh was at home, he usually crawled or slid around. He learned to think in terms of rationing leg use. He also began to glue bits of rubber and leather into his leg sockets as padding, to try to make them more comfortable.

He still didn't talk a lot to his family, but he was glad they were there around him.

Hugh called Bob one day to ask him to go to Rocks State Park.

"I have to work tomorrow, Hugh," he said. Bob had a job at a fast-food restaurant.

"What is this working bit? I don't get it," said Hugh. "You have to get your priorities straight, Bob."

"I'll have to meet you there later. Who's going?"

"Oh, the bros." Both Tony and Hans lived away from home now, but Hugh saw them often.

Bob arrived after the hour-long drive the next evening to find Hugh sitting in the car in the parking lot, listening to the radio.

"It's a long approach," Hugh said. He pointed out the right path. "Just go that way. You'll find 'em easily."

Bob didn't know whether he should go. But it seemed that was the only thing to do, and Hugh certainly expected him to. So he did. Hugh didn't appear sad, only passive.

———— • ————

News travels fast in the small world of climbers. As far away as Yosemite Valley, people discussed the accident and shook their heads, nodded, speculated, and second-guessed. One climber from the Adirondacks stood in the Yosemite parking lot and told others, "Everybody in New Hampshire, all the climbers, are really pissed at that guy. They went up there, made all kinds of mistakes, and got a rescuer killed. They blew it bad."

Said a young woman, Elaine Watkins, "He lost his legs? God. He didn't exactly get off scot-free, then." Other listeners walked off, hushed, with their various opinions.

In Lancaster, Hugh dreaded opening the mail. Dozens of letters still arrived – from New England, from the rest of the country. Some people berated him; some tried to comfort him; some religious zealots told him he was condemned.

When friends called or visited, he made an attempt to be positive. He complained only when he talked to his parents, and then only about specifics – about pains or the way his legs were fitting – never about the way in which his life had changed. He didn't want people to think he was anyone different from the old Hugh Herr.

When he told his mother about the pain, she would break down and cry. "I would give you my legs if I could," she said once.

"I don't know why I even complain to Mom," he confided to Tony. "There's no way anyone can help me. I'm really alone."

At first Hugh made some efforts to keep people from fetching and doing things for him. "No, I can get it myself," he'd say. But he capitulated more and more. "The macho stuff lasts only so long," he said as Bob got up to change the TV channel while they watched one afternoon.

In those first months, whenever Hugh went out, he tried his hardest not to limp.

———— • ————

Hugh fought the rages that would descend on him by going climbing. "I had a drive. I had hope for something," he said later. "That's what kept me up."

When he did roped climbs, he was partnered by his brothers or Bob Mullins. Hugh was elated by his rapid progress. The first time he tried the arduous traverse on a certain boulder at Safe Harbor, he thought he could never do it. A week later he cruised it, then did it again, and again.

He succeeded largely because of his mental state, his anger about the misjudgment that had led to the accident. Physically and technically, what he was doing now was extraordinarily difficult. Hugh's achievements were of the same magnitude as his energy level; he possessed a heightened focus and awareness born of discomfort and pain. Because of the surgery and trauma, doing anything required more energy and effort than ever before, but now he did more than he ever had. Hugh was in a frenzy.

He wanted his old life back, he wanted his friends back, he wanted to climb. But most of his anger and intensity was born of Albert Dow's death. Every time the subject came up – a letter, a passing reference, or a question – it cut him.

Among his physical problems was that with his artificial legs cinched on tightly, he couldn't bend his knees well because of the back of the plastic calf; he could no longer high-step to reach an elevated foothold. But when he loosened his legs to allow a greater angle of bending, they wobbled. He realized he could have either good suspension or good flexibility, but not both. He finally reached a happy medium by making and wearing Lycra tights. The elastic fabric helped hold his artificial limbs on. He also wore a converted ladies' girdle at the junction between his real legs and his prostheses.

Still, he was restricted when using footholds off to the side. When he swung his leg onto a foothold that was not directly beneath him, he could not always adjust the angle of his artificial foot to fit it, especially if the hold was horizontal. He also had to pull his body higher than another climber to use a given foothold. He couldn't rock onto it.

Nevertheless, he was improving fast. Because his weight had gone from 140 to 126 pounds, his strength-to-weight ratio, critical in rock climbing, had improved. When he realized the implications, he phoned Morris Hershoff and said, "This is gonna be an advantage! For every pound a climber loses, he can do one more pull-up. And I've lost fourteen pounds."

Now he knew that it was possible to return to where he had been.

One day as he was climbing at Safe Harbor, he was surprised by a sudden rush of bliss and relief. He was high: he wanted to dance, to twist and wave and shout. Three days later, another such emotional surge came over him. Those rushes began to visit him a few times a week. They were born of the realization that he was alive, not dead; that he would climb again; that he was now wide awake, not sleeping as he had been for the last few months. The physical pain, too, was changing. He would feel it, then it would suddenly lessen, even disappear altogether.

The surges might come to him when he was indoors or outside, but he was usually alone. In later years he could never get that feeling back. He came to believe that the state couldn't be reached through any mechanism other than such trauma as he had been through. Though he described these blissful rushes in physical terms—"It's like hitting yourself with a hammer: it feels so good when you stop"—they were very spiritual.

Hugh had been through so much physical and mental pain that it was exhilarating when even the smallest part was resolved by progress and acceptance. Still, he thought about the accident almost constantly, and cried almost every day. These were not tears of depression. The crying was a spontaneous occurrence, and felt as natural as any other physiological function, almost like eating.

Bouldering, he nearly always went to the places he considered the most degrading, where the climbing was the hardest and he'd become the most frustrated. He longed to get frustrated because he wanted to get better. He usually went by himself.

He lost control only once during those practice sessions. It was at Safe Harbor, when he found himself unable to do the boulder problems he used to do. He had a tantrum. He yelled and cried. He picked up rocks and threw them at the railroad tracks. But he wouldn't have done it if anyone else had been there.

———— • ————

He worked at his craft all summer, in the first months sticking to the boulders and rock faces around his home. When he did venture out, it was only to some obscure cliffs in West Virginia. He deliberately stayed away from the Shawangunks. He wanted to be climbing 5.10 by the time he went there.

When Hugh led his first 5.10, in West Virginia, his climbing partner couldn't follow it. John Rosenfeld looked up, narrowing his eyes, smiled, and said, "You *suck.*"

Hugh first returned to the Gunks in July 1982 with Hans, Ellen, and their friend Zoltan Farkas. That night, upon arriving, they drove out to the cabin where Morris Hershoff was summering. Excited about seeing their good friend, Hans and Zoltan hopped out of the car and started running up the hill.

Back in the car, Ellen sat with Hugh. He was still. She already knew from his tenseness how worried he was.

"I know, Huey," she said gently.

"I can barely get out of this car, much less walk up to that hut," he said. "How am I going to climb?" Now, for the first time since the night before the amputations, she saw tears spilling down his face and heard him sobbing. He had endured this ordeal very well, had been very brave, she thought. But she had sometimes worried that he hadn't grieved enough.

"I know how hard it is," she said. "We all have our problems, Huey."

"What problems do you have?" he asked, almost sulkily.

"You know about my problems." Ellen had struggled for years against the pull of anorexia nervosa and bulimia.

Softly, "I know."

"Those problems aren't as bad as yours," she said. "But I've seen you and I know you and you're going to get through this. I know you'll climb again, just as well as before." She hadn't always believed that, but she did tonight. She thought, "If anybody can, it'll be Hugh."

The next day, belayed by Morris, Hugh sailed up two 5.11s. That was the elite grade of the time, a rating most climbers only dreamed about.

"Aren't you excited to be climbing five-eleven again?" Morris asked him.

Said Hugh evenly, "No. I have much higher hopes."

But after that, to his dismay and disbelief, Hugh was benched. He had abraded his limb ends with all the walking. The skin was broken, showing several small sores. Hugh's emotions plummeted. He was both discouraged and furious. "Climbing is so hard for me," he thought. "And this is what I get from it?"

Instead of climbing, Hugh watched Hans hang-glide from a hill near the Gunks, in Ellenville. While Hans was in the air, Hugh sat on a hillside alone and disconsolate. Ellen and Zoltan were there at the launch site as well, but only Ellen approached him. She even got him to laugh at the sight of one pilot who landed ignominiously, bashing down hard.

Then all four piled into a car. Hans, Ellen, and Zoltan tried to adhere to their plans, despite Hugh's glumness, and headed into New Paltz for dinner at the Gay 90s restaurant.

"I'm glad you were here," Hans said quietly to Ellen as they entered the restaurant. "Maybe it's just the typical Herr male way. I knew he was hurting and didn't want to bring it up. What could I say? I didn't know what to say."

Hugh's next trip was with Bob. They had planned to leave on Friday afternoon, when Bob finished work, but Bob's mother pressed them to stay so that they could greet Bob's father, who was due home from a business trip. "You can leave in the morning," she said.

But half an hour after the father walked in the door, at nine, Hugh and Bob started out on their four-and-a-half-hour drive. "Um, Hugh really wants to leave, bad," Bob explained.

The two climbers arrived in New Paltz in the middle of the night and camped out near the cliffs at the Coxing Kill area. They slept in the back of the Herrs' big station wagon, on a gymnastics mat borrowed from school, which they pushed up against the front seat and out on the open tailgate. Around them on the mat were all their climbing gear, a cooler, and a piled-up rope ladder they'd brought for training. The air in the wagon smelled of the ketchup one of them had spilled on a wool hat.

In the morning Hugh pointed Bob in the direction of Morris's cabin, to see whether his friend would like to come to the diner with them. Morris heard Bob's footsteps in the leaves as he approached.

"Hey, can you, uh, open the door?" he called.

"Sure," said Bob politely, wondering why Morris couldn't do that himself.

Morris explained. The night before, some campers had been noisy, and the cabin door wouldn't stay shut, so he had stuffed a stick into the latch to keep it closed. The trick had worked rather too well.

Later that day, on a moderate climb, Hugh got a foot stuck in a crack. He kicked and scrabbled around but couldn't yank it out. He finally placed a piece of protection, clipped a sling into it and his harness, and hung on the piece while he worked on retrieving the foot. Bob didn't laugh until he heard Hugh chuckling.

The two stayed in the Gunks for two weeks. One day they had to hitchhike back from the Skytop cliff, located on private land to which car access is restricted. Hugh put on his most pathetic face as they waited for a ride. Bob stood back from the road. "Take a leg off, come on," he said. "Then they'll really stop." But Hugh wouldn't oblige.

At the end of each day of climbing, Hugh would say in a mock-heroic voice, "And they lived to tell the story one more time."

At home, when Bob came over to the Herrs' house, Hugh's father sometimes asked him about school and his plans for college. Bob was to be starting at Millersville, a state university, in the autumn. John Herr would then try to convince Hugh that college was different from high school. "You might like it," he said.

Hugh never took it very seriously. "School's not everything," he teased. "There are other things in life."

"Climbing's not everything," Bob replied smartly. "There's school."

———————— • ————————

In September 1982, Hugh returned to high school for his senior year. He wasn't glad to be going back. This was just something he had to do.

"I'll be a chameleon," he thought. "I'll be whatever the situation is. I'll adapt to everything, including this."

But the first day he walked into school, he was afraid. As he entered his first class, he knew that everyone was looking at him. His classmates' faces showed surprise, even shock. They had thought he would be in a wheelchair. The other students all knew what had occurred, but no one said anything that revealed any awareness. It was almost, in fact, as if nothing had ever happened.

One of the few people who didn't know about the accident was Hugh's science teacher. On a sunny day in September he took the class outside to a field where they could look for insects. Hugh kept tripping over vines and finally just lay down in the middle of the field and dug there. His teacher came up and said, "What's wrong with you?"

Hugh said, "I have artificial legs." He got up and marched stiffly back to the classroom. Oddly, as much as anything, he was angry that he hadn't been able to find any bugs.

His limb ends continued to shrink. During the nights, however, his legs swelled up, and he had to walk on them first thing in the morning to get to school. Then, when he sat down for classes, the legs would swell again. Some days the pain was so bad he could barely keep from screaming; one day tears ran down his face as he sat at his desk. He had to take Tylenol, which he hated. He hated any drug.

But he always had his other focus. By October his days had fallen into a schedule. He attended his three academic classes in the morning, then skipped lunch and drove the rusty Dodge out to Eshleman, the stone elementary school a mile away. There he would boulder for half an hour or an hour, until it was time to go to the machine shop at the nearby vocational-technical school. After work at the machine shop, he usually went bouldering again.

He could by now do many hours of hard climbing. But he could get a sore from walking for five minutes if his legs weren't fitting right.

Hugh needed his acrylic legs replaced at regular intervals because of limb shrinkage, which is affected by time, diet, and activity. Each week he drove to Philadelphia to see his prosthetist, Frank Malone.

"I've lost my legs, not my mind," Hugh thought. "I still have the knowledge and mind-set of a hard rock climber. I still know how to position my body on hard rock walls. I need devices, I need mechanical contrivances that will allow me to connect my physical world with everything I can conceive of doing."

Under Frank's tutelage, Hugh began working on his artificial legs himself. He made an important realization: that he should not confuse his own foot capabilities with those of human feet. He didn't need to replicate the legs he'd lost; he could work with whole new shapes and possibilities. Having decided that, he began to think of being disabled

LANCASTER COUNTY, PENNSYLVANIA   H H

as only a temporary condition. Disadvantages, he thought excitedly, could be wiped out simply by a change in prosthetic design.

"I am not handicapped," he thought, "the prosthetic technology is."

He made feet of different sizes and shapes. Some had pointed toes for cracks, and others were for edges. He put climbing-shoe rubber on them and ground it down. He tried to make an ankle that flexed, but it never worked.

As he'd grown up, Hugh had read the Bible somewhat regularly, out of philosophical as much as spiritual interest. But now he stopped. He became solely analytical: calculating, problem-solving, caught up in causes and effects. He no longer thought, "There's magic out there."

———— • ————

The autumn he went back to school Hugh could climb much better than he could walk. He used his hands often on walls, palming as he walked; he touched the tabletops in the Plaza Diner as he moved stiffly past them.

He always rode a bicycle to the base of climbs. Taking advantage of the many roads and good trails in the Shawangunks, Hugh would get as close to his routes as possible, then stash his bicycle in the woods. Someone coming along behind him might also find, a bit farther, a pair of ski poles or crutches hidden among the boulders.

He went straight back to doing first ascents, attempting stretches of rock no one had climbed. Working on one new route in the Skytop ridge, he took a fall that spun him sideways into the wall with a smack. One of his feet cracked off and thudded down to the talus below, bouncing off a rock.

The Skytop cliffs are near an opulent 280-room hotel, whose guests frequently walk along trails just below the cliffs and watch the climbers.

"Hey!" Hugh called to a hiker. "Would you grab that shoe down there?"

The man scrambled across boulders to retrieve it. A moment later, tremulous tones floated up: "There's something in it." The pink rubber foot was still inside.

Hugh stowed the broken foot in his pack. Then Bob and another friend helped him hobble back along the trail to the hotel, where he could wait for a car. A woman rushed out. "Do you need a doctor?" she asked.

"He's O.K.," said Bob, straight-faced. "We'll just take him to the body shop."

Hugh named the route *Footloose and Fancy Free.*

Later, *Accidents in North American Mountaineering*, normally a serious-minded publication, reported the incident: ". . . a hold broke. He fell three meters to the ground and had to be taken to the factory, as his artificial legs were in need of repair."

Hugh was given a new nickname, Mechanical Boy. He responded by giving that name to another of his first ascents.

Stories about him spread anew, and Hugh was much admired and praised, especially among the Gunks climbers. He was, to outward appearances, riding high. People teased and twitted him, a sure sign of acceptance.

At the home of his friends Laura Chaitin and Rosie Andrews, Hugh lay on the floor. "Laura, would you hand me a cookie?" he asked. He looked up to see Laura towering above him, wagging a finger.

"You just take those legs off and then don't move, don't you?" she scolded in mock exasperation.

Hugh later had a more serious talk with Rosie. He told her about waking up after his surgery, and what it was like to look down at his short legs for the first time. Rosie–a particularly good, perceptive listener–was surprised and flattered that he expressed so much.

Despite the pride and pleasure he enjoyed in his life at the Gunks, Hugh was aware of the real reason he was climbing so many new routes, but he shared it with no one.

He was afraid to try any established climbs–routes that he would formerly have done with few or no falls–because he was afraid to fall on them or fail to get up altogether. His ego, he recognized, was both huge and fragile. All that autumn, he lived a kind of duality. He was joyous and took an innocent pleasure in showing off, in receiving praise. Conversely, he also felt furtive, like an impostor: though climbing beyond people's expectations, he knew he wasn't as good as they thought he was. He could do some hard climbs, but not others. He did not consider himself solid in the 5.11 grade, and he was too scared to find out what his limits were.

The accident was still always on his mind, through fall and winter. It didn't recede and then come back; it was just there, in the recesses of his consciousness, daily.

He was fairly accustomed to his new body, but occasionally something surprised him. Crawling along at home one day, he suddenly caught sight of himself in a mirror and was startled.

It saddened him profoundly to look at other people who had missing limbs. He felt much sorrier for them than for himself. There was much more acceptance when he looked down at his own body, just because it was his own.

Sometimes in a store window he watched himself walking and thought, "God, that's weird." He would test the image by trying to walk the very best he could. But his body leaned far forward, and his gait was awkward.

Whenever he got fed up, or when his legs weren't fitting right, he would go to the phone, call someone, and talk about climbing. "He can go from a long, long face to being on top of the world," his mother said to Tony. "You should see our phone bills."

Hugh's self-consciousness faded toward the end of winter. By then he didn't usually care what people noticed.

———— • ————

In the spring of 1983 Hugh appeared on the cover of *Outside* magazine, sitting on a boulder, his own legs extended, wearing his artificial legs, but with no feet attached to them. His different pairs of climbing and walking feet surrounded him. The feature profile within wondered whether there had ever been another top athlete who had lost an essential body part but returned to the cutting edge of his sport.

Hugh's first reaction on seeing the cover shot was both delight and irritation. "I *knew* they'd do that," he thought, "show me with my feet off."

That article and many others inspired a new kind of correspondence. "My eyes are blue, my hair is brown, my measurements are 34-24-34 . . ." wrote one girl. Others sent photos and handmade gifts.

After receiving a photo of yet another admirer, Hugh looked at his mother with affected resignation and said, "I have a lot of problems." He laughed giddily.

Tidying up one day, his mother found a stray letter and skimmed it. "It seems as if the girl writing it is an amputee, too, Hugh," she said. "I think you ought to answer her."

Hugh looked at the letter and couldn't remember whether he had replied or not. He sighed. "Those Nevada girls keep me so busy," he said. He was beginning to forget his fears that women would avoid him.

———— • ————

When, late that winter, he eventually began to try the established routes again, Hugh was mortified to think that he might fail. But during the act of climbing, as he focused on moves and strategies, he found that his mind lifted into the same exalted state it used to, in which he did not worry about failure. He relished the difficulty and uncertainty. He had always felt guilty, even deadened, when things weren't hard.

He was soon ticking off the various Gunks testpieces again, often attracting little knots of watchers. Hugh was used to that. People had always watched him, previously because he was so young. When he wasn't climbing his best, he didn't like having an audience; when he was climbing well, he loved it.

He began to make his own clothes in flamboyant colors and styles, in the Lycra that had first held his legs on. Although such dress later became common, in the early 1980s most climbers were still fairly muted, likely to wear baggy clothes of navy blue and forest green. Hugh's garb was electric. He began to dress up every time he climbed, and frequently when he didn't. The style was his way of celebrating life and expressing his pride in his ability to climb again, and in his individuality. He enjoyed his clothes' shock value; he wanted to be wild. He wanted to have fun.

The clothes became an integral part of his climbing psyche. He had a very different attitude when he was wearing bright colors than when he looked down and saw old jeans.

He still had a great dread of failing, and if he didn't think his feet were technically perfect, he lost his momentum. But if his feet were right and he was wearing Lycra pants, he felt that there was no stopping him.

He still didn't want anybody to think of him as handicapped. "I am handicapped," he thought, "but not in rock climbing." He couldn't envision himself in any substandard terms. "So I've just gotten so good that it doesn't matter," he explained to Tony. "I don't have to accept that I'm not as good anymore because I *am*. Most amputees have to accept a profound physical disability. But in my vertical world, my legs rarely hold me back."

———— • ————

Only at the very end of Hugh's senior year did one student make any reference to the accident. The young man was most concerned. "Hugh," he said, lowering his voice, "did you get frostbite on your penis?"

Hugh said, "No," and tried not to laugh.

The classmate bridled defensively. "You know that happens, don't you?" he asked.

Though many of his exchanges with students remained fairly monosyllabic, Hugh was noticing changes in his own attitude. Formerly, without making much effort, he had been well liked. His combination of shyness and self-possession, his sweet and easy manner, and his reputation as a gymnast had been enough to attract girls. He, however, had been somewhat indifferent. No girlfriend had interested him nearly as much as climbing.

Now, since his accident, he had become less detached. He found that he actually liked people—his classmates, various friends, various fellow climbers. It was turning out to be a fun year.

His parents noticed that he was becoming more gregarious, much more outspoken. Whereas Hugh in conversation had once been mostly reactive, now he took the initiative far oftener, elaborated beyond abbreviated answers, even asked questions. During the last year he had been given a great deal of practice in verbal interaction. In the hospital he'd had to speak up to his caretakers for what he wanted; he'd had to give interviews and receive visitors.

Hugh's accident had brought him down; now he was bringing himself back up. It was like making the second ascent of a difficult route, working hard for it, being thrilled by it, knowing it is possible. There was a difference, though. Usually a second ascent is easier than the first, for that same reason—the climber knows the route is possible, as someone has been there before. But no one had ever climbed Hugh's route.

13

It was early in the summer of 1983, and Hugh had just graduated. Thirty feet up a rock wall, he pressed down with three fingertips on a small edge and reached right to pinch a vertical projection, his thumb opposing on a sloping pebble. He moved his feet up on two edges and slapped with his left hand to palm a dent in the rock, then reached right to a small square edge. His last piece of protection was well below his feet. His left hand crossed over his right to get a good edge. He pulled up to a table-sized flat ledge and whooped.

His pants were purple with white stripes, and he wore a leopard-spotted vest over a shiny, multicolored shirt. His chalk was contained in an upside-down teddy bear fastened at his waist.

One by one, he brought three other climbers up the route; they all took falls but eventually joined him. A fourth, his strength spent, gave up halfway.

Hugh rappelled to the ground. He rested his left hand on his knee, took an Allen wrench from his pack, inserted it into a hole in the bottom of his foot, and unscrewed the appendage. Made of wood and rubber, it was painted in a parody of a Nike sneaker. The fiberglass leg was blue, decorated with pink polka dots. He mentioned to one of his partners that he had tried to climb this route, a direct finish to his own *Sticky Bun Power*, which he'd ascended three years before.

"But I was doing it all wrong then," he said, pulling from his pack a checkered shoe and a purple walking foot three sizes larger than the one he had just removed. "It's all in the footwork."

———— • ————

That summer the television show *Real People* made a film about Hugh. A camera crew came to his house in Lancaster and filmed him as he took one of the show's regulars, Sarah Purcell, to a small local cliff, Chickie's Rock. The cameramen also filmed him training in the family's barn, doing eight straight one-arm pull-ups.

Then the entourage drove north to the Gunks, where they hired Russ Clune and Russ Raffa to help set up ropes and lower and raise people and equipment. Bob Carmichael, an independent filmmaker, was the producer. Hugh's climbing partner was Tony.

During the two days on location, the pair climbed a host of hard classics: *Foops, Scare City, Super Crack*, and *Crack of Bizarre Delights*. Hugh climbed *Foops* six times for the cameras.

He and Tony had never talked much when they were climbing, but Bob Carmichael wanted them to speak to each other. "Act supportive," he said.

They were hardly polished actors. "Go for it," Hugh said in a monotone.

"Yeah. All right."

Finally, on one route Hugh got excited and carried away and started spouting Gunks slang. "Bone the piss—yeah! Now go for the volcanic board!" he exulted as Tony pulled up on a small hold and reached for a big one.

"Huey," ordered Russ Clune through cupped hands. "*Stop talking.*"

Other Gunks friends, who drifted toward the film crew at various times during the day, noticed what Hugh's parents had observed. Rosie Andrews couldn't believe Hugh's assurance. "He's like a little movie star," she said, amused.

That night, the crew wanted some footage of Hugh out on the town, having fun with his friends. The gang entered the Bacchus restaurant, whose downstairs bar scene was in full swing. From a table, Hugh began watching a slender, sweet-faced waitress. She had dark hair pulled back into a ponytail, and an artless, unself-conscious manner. "Boy," he said to Bob Carmichael. "Isn't she cute?"

Carmichael leaned back and gazed across the room, too. Then he said, "I'm going to go talk to her." Hugh tittered. Carmichael marched across the room and approached the waitress.

"My name is Bob Carmichael," he said. "I'm a filmmaker. We're wondering if you'd come dance with this guy."

The girl looked over at Hugh and smiled shyly. She knew who he was."O.K.," she said. Bob put out his hand, and she shook it. "My name's Lenore." He led her across the floor for an introduction. She danced with Hugh for a segment of the film.

In the days and weeks that followed, Lenore became Hugh's first girlfriend in a year and a half.

———— • ————

Russ Clune and Russ Raffa wanted to go climbing in North Conway and urged Hugh to come. He hesitated only a little. "There's no better time," he thought, "and no better way than to go with these two." He packed up his rope and gear, his four pairs of climbing feet, and his garish clothes.

On the steep granite of the 450-foot Cathedral Ledge, the three started in right away on the 5.12s. Russ Clune did *White Eye* but failed on *The Possessed*, and Hugh pulled off *The Possessed* but swung off the strenuous traverse on *White Eye*. Russ Raffa got up both climbs. "So we both hate him," Hugh said to Clune.

The most dramatic item on their agenda, however, was the aid route *Tourist Treat*, a winding path up the main wall of the cliff, wire-brushed clean of the lichen that covered much of that section, and for that reason the most obvious line on the cliff. Many climbers had tried the route, but no one had free-climbed it.

As the three Gunkies took turns on *Tourist Treat*, Paul Ross, one of the Mountain Rescue team, watched from the top of the Prow, a large formation nearby. Each of the three would reach the *Tourist Treat* crux, place his left pinky in a small sharp fingerlock, stretch his right arm far to the next slot, and then try to wriggle his left foot high into a pod and reach higher for edges.

"Hugh was getting the highest," Ross told friends afterward. "Then each time he fell off, he'd tape up his little finger." Here Ross assumed a look of resignation and disgust, winding imaginary tape around his little finger. "Go up, come down, put on tape; go up, come down, put on tape."

When Doug Madara, one of the four searchers who had climbed up Odell's to look for Jeff and Hugh, first saw Hugh that same afternoon, he was struck chiefly by his pink and purple clothes. For a second Doug thought Hugh was a clown from the carnival that was in town, then realized who it was.

Walking down the street the next morning, Hugh wondered whether the people he passed might have been out looking for him during the snowstorm. He entered a popular breakfast diner, the Big Pickle, and sat with Russ Clune and Russ Raffa. The Pickle was packed with a moving, shifting mix of locals, anglers, and climbers, all eating pancakes and over-easies and three-egg omelettes. Waitresses rushed between the counter and the small tables, carrying coffee pots.

As Doug Madara walked by on his way to a table, Russ Clune leaned back and greeted him warmly. "Dougie, how you doing?" He turned to gesture at his young friend. "Have you met Huey?"

Madara thought, "No, but I sure spent a lot of time trying to." He reached across the table to shake hands. "How are you?" he said. "Glad to meet you."

Hugh met several other locals that morning. He felt cautious and was sensitive to people's reactions, but everyone seemed friendly and natural. He was introduced to Marc Chauvin, another searcher, by a mutual acquaintance. "Do you guys know each other?" the friend asked.

"No, but I think I can guess who you are," Chauvin said, smiling and holding out his hand.

———————•———————

Hugh's appearance sparked various conversations, assessments, and questions. Some people were as undisturbed as Paul Ross, others not. One woman walked into the International Mountaineering Equipment store that day, saw Hugh sitting on a chair and flipping through a guidebook, and wondered resentfully, "What's *he* doing here?"

During a Big Pickle breakfast, Elaine Watkins, a climbing instructor who was new in town, asked Michael Hartrich about the area climate in the wake of the accident. He spoke candidly.

"People were upset," Hartrich said. "Around here there tend to be two camps – people you know and people you don't. The boys did things most people wouldn't have done. But they didn't do anything I haven't done. I just didn't do them all at once."

"How did you feel?" she asked.

"I felt more upset with the press. Such a hullaballoo. They got hold of it and threw it around. Something out west wouldn't warrant the coverage this did. Avalanches are more newsworthy for New England."

"How did people feel about the press later, the stories about his comeback?"

"People were upset when articles didn't point out the mistakes the boys made, that they were lucky to be alive."

She asked about the conditions during the rescue. "For an experienced climber they weren't extraordinary," Hartrich said. "The terrain was not very difficult technically. I don't think anybody felt they were sticking their necks out.

"People can say to me, 'You and Albert shouldn't have been there,' but that's hindsight. You have only so much information at the time. You can't sit around and dig snow pits and look at them for half an hour. There was avalanche danger above, but it didn't seem that bad where we were."

Hartrich accepted a refill of coffee. "It was chance that Albert hit a tree. If he'd ended up like me, one of us might have dug the other out. We'd have brushed ourselves off and laughed about it."

Around town, a pattern emerged. The people who were most critical tended to be locals who were nonclimbers, or climbers from out of town. Most of the Mountain Rescue Service members, the men who had gone out in the blizzard, were accepting of Hugh's presence.

Said Paul Ross from his home on the riverbank in Conway, "Certainly I don't resent Hugh and Jeff. People don't get rescued because they're out there enjoying themselves. They get rescued because they need help.

"There but for the grace of God goes any of us," he said. "We've all made mistakes. It's just that the rest of us didn't get caught." In Ross's home country, Great Britain, bad weather and rescues are common, and even rescue tragedies are accepted.

"I've been lost," he added. "When I was very young, about sixteen or seventeen, I used to go blundering up mountains. Once I had to walk fourteen miles to get home. I never got bloody lost again, I can tell you!"

———— • ————

Hugh returned to the Gunks for his next several weekends. On one such visit, he and Russ Clune heard that Lynn Hill, a Californian and the best woman climber in the country–perhaps the world–was in town. She arrived at the cliffs, and as she roped up to do the classic 5.10-plus testpiece *Matinee*, Russ, Tony, and Hugh settled themselves on a ledge opposite to watch. She cruised the route and they began to stir, ready to do something themselves.

All fired up, Hugh suggested a line just next to them, attempted during a recent visit by Mike "Claw" Law, one of Australia's leading climbers. The theatrical Law, who had been the earliest inspiration for Hugh's present sartorial inclinations, had dubbed it *Kinky Claw*. It was known to be hard and unprotected.

Hugh motored up the climb, tried to place protection and couldn't, and made the decision to keep going. Tony, below, thought he had never seen his brother so on the edge, yet still on. Hugh was lunging, slapping.

Now, if he fell, he would hit the deck. Both Russ and Tony looked at each other and turned their faces away. Tony fed the rope out by feel. "It's worse to be a belayer than the leader," Tony thought. "It's like being a passenger in a car during a snowstorm: the driver is so busy concentrating, he worries less."

Above, Hugh had figured that he needed to do four more moves, one of them difficult, to reach a good horizontal. He didn't think he'd hit the ground, though he did consider that he might hit a ledge if he fell. Still, he judged that the hard move in front of him wasn't as bad as everyone thought. He bet it was only 5.11-minus. And even if he fell from that, he wouldn't hit the ledge. Falling from the 5.10 section above the next move would have a different outcome, but he considered such a fall unlikely.

He made it to the top. And though Tony thought the risk too high, he respected what it had taken for Hugh to finish the climb. It was more than another first ascent, however, Tony thought. It was a milestone. It was the first time since the accident that Hugh had gone all out.

Hugh considered this milestone unremarkable. His attitude toward pure rock climbing had remained essentially unaffected during his rehabilitation and comeback. To him, the accident had nothing to do with rock climbing. The accident had been about being lost, about being trapped in deep snow in a forest. The dangers specific to rock climbing did not bother him, and the only factor he had considered during the ascent was the presence of the crowd, which had made him feel more keen and determined. What would bother him was walking in snow.

"So how was it?" Lynn asked.

Hugh was his usual self. "It was O.K.," he said.

———— • ————

Russ Clune and Hugh returned to North Conway a month later and stayed for three days at Elaine Watkins's apartment. Russ had met Elaine out west several years before, and they had climbed together a few times.

One night Russ and Hugh took their hostess out to dinner at the Oxen Yoke restaurant in North Conway. Curious, as people always were, she asked Hugh all about himself. Russ listened patiently.

When Hugh said solemnly, "I've got the youngest ascents of both *Kansas City* and *Super Crack*," Russ taunted him.

"Oh, Huey, you're *so* great," Russ said. Hugh guffawed.

Hugh later minutely described the moves – every flake, nubbin, and fingerlock – on a particular route that he had done years before.

"I can't believe how well you remember it," Elaine remarked.

"I remember the moves on every climb I've ever done," Hugh said. Russ nodded reflectively, idly fingering the cloth napkin lining a breadbasket.

Moments later the two began to argue about whether Hugh would ever be as good a climber now as he would have been otherwise.

"You probably won't," Russ said.

Hugh debated spiritedly, citing his strength-to-weight ratio, his mechanical tricks. After a few minutes, he said, "It's stupid to ask, would I have been better? The proper question is, am I going to get better? You have to look at reality, how I was climbing then, and how I'm climbing now." He shook his head in confident dismissal.

A moment later a new idea made him burst out laughing. "You know what I'm going to do next time I'm at the Gunks? Put my feet on backward, with the toes sticking out behind me, and stand on Main Street in front of David's Cookies eating an ice cream cone. Just to see people's faces."

It was pouring rain outside, and Hugh and Elaine stood in a doorway while Russ brought the car around from the parking lot. She looked at Hugh and at the raindrops and thought, "So many tears."

Hugh said, sighing, "I'm so tired."

"But you didn't climb much today, did you? What time did the rain start?"

"Oh, no, it's not the climbing. It's just that I can't ever sleep."

She waited, not knowing what to think.

"I can't sleep, thinking about all the climbs I want to do," he said. He paused. The rain pattered on leaves all around. "Sometimes I'm lying in bed at night and I get the feeling there's nothing I can't climb. I couldn't love any other sport as much as climbing. I love the gymnastics of it. But in gymnastics, you work on one move, over and over, and then do it in competition. In climbing, you're usually doing it on-sight. It could never possibly get boring."

Back at the apartment half an hour later, Russ was stretched out in a comfortable position on the worn carpet. He jerked his thumb toward Hugh. "He isn't really interested in other things. Well, movies and rock music, but everybody's interested in those." Hugh shrugged.

At the cliffs the next day, Elaine fell into conversation about Hugh with another climber, Carl, an instructor for Eastern Mountain Sports. Carl said he saw Hugh's alleged advantages—better strength-to-weight ratio, different feet—as something else. "He's cheating!" he exclaimed.

She was truly surprised. "Are you kidding?" she asked hesitantly. "No, I'm not kidding," he said, agitated. "That's aid." Although aid usually means pulling on a sling or carabiner, it can mean any other suspect tactics. "All those different kinds of feet he has," Carl said. "That's aid."

With some trepidation, Elaine later repeated the exchange. To her surprise, Hugh laughed. To him such an argument meant that he was finally fully accepted, considered a real competitor, and given no allowances.

———— • ————

Hugh went back to climbing in the Shawangunks for the rest of the summer. He and Lenore drifted apart, although they remained friends. Hugh was to have a similar problem with women again and again: he didn't give them enough time. He put his climbing above the relationship, and when his girlfriends realized that, they left.

In late summer Tony and Morris Hershoff joined Hugh for his first road trip since the accident, a five-week tour of Colorado. It was a triumph. A postcard was delivered to the Rock and Snow shop in New Paltz, addressed to a friend who had requested a progress report. "O.K., Laura, here's your stupid immature list," Hugh wrote impishly. He listed more than twenty 5.11s and 5.12s he had climbed, including the 5.12-plus *Cinch Crack*.

On the same trip, however, he was finding out his inconsistencies. One day he, Tony, and their longtime friend Alex Lowe went climbing together, and Hugh set off to do the first pitch of the 5.10 route *XM*. Tony and Alex lolled at the base, both talking of climbing trips they'd taken to India. The initial crack was 5.8 and considered an offwidth, or wide crack; the usual way to ascend it would have been by pressing a heel on one side and toes against the other. Hugh placed one good piece of protection, a sling around a rock horn, and moved above it. Having difficulty with the heel-toe sections, he moved outside the chimney and worked upward on down-sloping holds on the adjacent walls. But suddenly his feet skidded and exploded off the bad holds.

Alex, below, was belaying only casually as he and Tony chatted; it never occurred to him that Hugh would have trouble with a 5.8 pitch.

Suddenly there was a rustling, clanking sound as Hugh ripped downward. Yanked by the rope, Alex slammed against the wall before Hugh came to the end of his thirty-foot ride, upside-down.

There was a moment of stunned silence, followed by a few are-you-all-rights. Hugh looked at Alex and saw he was barely keeping a straight face. Fuming and embarrassed, Hugh went back up and led the pitch.

In the midst of the joys of having the freedom to travel and climb, Hugh was realizing more precisely than he had before how much he was not going to be able to do. He was learning what it would mean to live not months or even years but a lifetime of pain.

One day Hugh, Tony, and Morris set out for the Eldorado Canyon floor outside Boulder to do some routes on the higher West Ridge. As they were packing ropes, Hugh realized he could not go because he could not make the half-hour walk to the cliff. He stayed in the car at the parking lot all day.

A few days later, when the three arrived for breakfast at the L.A. Diner, Hugh remained seated in the car. He was fiddling with his bits of leather, padding his sockets. "Huey's sniffin' glue again," Morris teased. He and Tony went ahead.

Inside, they got their coffee but waited for Hugh before ordering. Ten minutes went by, then twenty. Tony became irritated and concerned. He went out to the car and found his brother sobbing. "Hugh . . . what?" he asked.

"The pain," was Hugh's only explanation.

Tony's face softened. "You should have *told* me," he said. "We've been sitting in there waiting."

"You don't know."

Tony sighed. "No, I don't know," he said. "But please, just talk to me about it, O.K.?"

Tony later called his wife from a pay phone. When he mentioned that Morris and Hugh were hoping to extend the trip by a few days, Sally did not object. "Oh, stay another week," she said.

Tony's next climbing trip was to be a visit to Rio de Janeiro with Russ Clune. Although Sally was included, she didn't want to go, and in deference to her, Tony agreed to stay home. But when he saw Russ

Clune at the Gunks the following weekend, Russ's enthusiasm prevented Tony from telling him. Tony wanted to go, always had.

The first thing Sally said when he walked in the door that Sunday night was, "Did you tell him?"

Tony didn't answer directly. "Don't you want to go, Sally?" he asked. "We'd have a great time."

She didn't answer.

———— • ————

That fall the *National Enquirer* printed an interview with Hugh and paid him three hundred dollars for ten minutes on the phone. The article was filled with dreamily religious lines. Hugh was also quoted as saying that from his niche between two rocks in the Great Gulf, "I looked up and saw the most beautiful girl I'd ever seen."

Reading it, Russ Clune roared with laughter. "Huey," he said, "you whore."

"You know what?" said Hugh. "I don't even remember what she looked like."

"Why in the world did you do that interview?"

"Out of perverse curiosity," said Hugh. "I wanted to see how the story would come out, how much it would be botched. Turns out, more than I expected. It was fiction."

"Did you ever even mention religion?"

"No," Hugh said.

By winter his mother had saved a ten-inch stack of newspapers and magazines containing articles about Hugh. The Associated Press story was published across the nation and around the world. One climber from North Conway saw it in Nairobi.

Hugh had an uncle in Kenya who was living alone and working a three-year stint as a Mennonite missionary, teaching farming and building in a remote area. One night he happened to stay up until midnight, which was unusual for him; that night he turned on his radio, which was equally uncharacteristic. As soon as he flicked it on, he heard the familiar tones of Paul Harvey on *Voice of America* telling the story of a boy from Pennsylvania. It was about Hugh.

Other accounts appeared in *Yankee, Reader's Digest*, the *Provi-*

dence Journal Sunday Magazine, Germany's *Stern,* the *Washington Post Magazine, Country America,* and even the elementary school publication *The Weekly Reader.*

Hugh found that getting press led him to want more. He began to see, in his interactions with people, that being well known brought its own kind of power. A person who is known, he thought, is given more opportunities than someone else. Any opportunities and fortune that fell into his lap could compensate for the loss of privacy.

Constantly told he was good, Hugh was finding it hard to keep a level attitude. But he tried to be sensitive, to keep from becoming big-headed. He had seen climbing heroes rudely, hurtfully dismiss people who tried to talk to them, and he determined not to go that route. He also believed that arrogance made a person lazy, made him stop trying.

Still, he was aware that the more recognition came his way, the more he wanted. His attitudes, in some ways, became more selfish. Publicity became the same thing as approval.

Hugh's friends in the Shawangunks started to wonder openly about his renown. Said Barbara Devine, "People are so fickle. What about when Huey isn't so hot, and they find someone else to worship?"

Dan McMillan reflected, "I really love Huey, and it's difficult to criticize him. Around the Gunks people admire what he's done so much, they think he can do no wrong. I see him capitalizing on that, getting people to belay him on the climbs he wants to do.

"He's completely self-confident, completely self-contained. He doesn't drop names of climbs like the rest of us do. Most people manage to work it into conversation that they've done this or that route. Hugh doesn't need to. He doesn't cut down or belittle other climbers, either."

Hugh had never been one to denigrate other climbers, but now he never voiced even the slightest criticism. After his accident everyone had been judging every aspect of his life. Now he took a nonjudgmental attitude to its extreme.

But, Dan said to a journalist, "I think he is isolating himself. He's a monomaniac. It's sick. I think an obsession with climbing, work, whatever, is selfish. You may get to be the best or the most recognized, but it seems warped. I like the idea of many interests."

Hugh, reading the comments, responded. "There will always be critics. I find it depressing to think about anyone who has no one thing he loves passionately. I think the person who's just O.K. at a lot of things is missing something. Those people are just touching things. To be the best demands everything.

"I enjoy extracting every inch out of life," Hugh said. "It means looking closely at the world and at myself."

Said his father to a friend one night, "If he ever wants to become a millionaire, watch out."

———— • ————

Jeff Batzer had returned to his work as a machinist and learned to play the guitar. He lectured to church and youth groups in the Northeast about mountain safety and religious faith. Lacking fingertips, Jeff did not return to climbing, but he did again take up competitive cycling. At the end of summer, he completed a bicycle race up Mount Washington.

The race announcer gave the spectators a brief account of the accident on the mountain. When Jeff crossed the finish line, he got a standing ovation.

He and Hugh had drifted apart since the accident, mainly because they no longer had climbing in common, but he called Hugh afterward to tell him about the race. They were both proud.

———— • ————

Autumn 1983 was Hugh's best season yet. Having again climbed the 5.12-plus *Super Crack*, he now climbed up it, and down, and up again, doing laps.

He, Russ Clune, Jeff Gruenwald, and Lynn Hill—an elite corps—made the first ascent of a long-term project they named *Vandals*. Weeks of working on each move culminated when three of them managed to finish it on one day; Hill succeeded the following week.

"It's the hardest thing I've ever done, anywhere in the world," said Clune. He knew it was 5.13, one of the country's first few at that grade.

One night a week later, Hugh was walking down the street alone in New Paltz when he ducked into an alley, looking for a place to sit while he adjusted his artificial legs. He found a trash can. Just as he sat down, a small window above his head lit up, filling the black alley with light. Seconds later, music from the room filled Hugh's ears. It was the Police song, "Sending out an SOS," that he and Jeff had heard all the way to Mount Washington. The music and the pain made him sob.

In October Hugh started making Lycra pants at home in characteristically wild colors and patterns. The pants became the big trend for hot climbers: Russ Clune had some, Rosie Andrews had some, and soon everybody was wearing them.

He also began giving slide shows for the handicapped; even blind people came. In his presentations he recounted what had happened to him and Jeff, and to Albert Dow, on Mount Washington. He described the rescue and the mistakes he and Jeff had made, and said simply that because of frostbite his lower legs had been amputated.

"I stand here now supported by carbon fiber, titanium, and steel, not by human means," he said. "Without my artificial legs, I would not be able to get out of bed in the morning.

"But the fact that I am handicapped is only a temporary condition. I am dependent on a technology—but that technology is limitless in potential."

He described how he thought of his artificial limbs as an advantage: "My dream—not just to rehabilitate myself, but to extend beyond the human limit—has become a reality. The fact that I am able to climb better with artificial legs is a glimpse into the future.

"If someone tomorrow designed me a leg that would allow me to run and jump, then I would run and jump. Just as a race-car driver is able to win because of a better car, I would be able to run and leap better because of improvements in prosthetic technology.

"It's not true that you have to 'live with it.' All you have to do is figure out how to rehabilitate yourself. Physical disabilities can be overcome through technical means. Someday, when technology is advanced enough, people will no longer be physically disabled."

When he was with other climbers, however, his explanations of the advantages he perceived were concrete. "I'm lighter," he said. "I can do more pull-ups. My feet are smaller."

These days, Hugh's goals related only to climbing; the obsessed don't see well outside their capsules. "I just want to take more climbing trips," he told a reporter. College would be fun but a waste of time. "I'd rather get my pants and slide-show businesses going, and climb," he told his friend Neil Cannon, a New Hampshire climber and graduate student at Dartmouth. He also sometimes spoke of getting exposure and sponsorship.

"I want to climb a big peak," he told Neil. "It's not as interesting as rock climbing, but it would be a bigger challenge. It'd be the ultimate."

"What about carrying loads?" Neil asked.

"There're always Sherpas," Hugh said blithely. "Wouldn't it be great to do Everest? Think of the sponsors. I'd get a hold of Nike and say I want to do the first sneaker ascent."

Real People flew Hugh to Hollywood for a studio appearance that would air with the climbing footage they had shot in Lancaster and the Shawangunks. Dressed in trademark style, Hugh strolled onstage to the sound of the huge audience clapping and cheering. He bowed and waved, and raised both arms above his head in a victory cheer.

Some viewers, however, found Hugh's enthusiasm to be self-aggrandizing. A woman from Manchester, New Hampshire, wrote a pained, emotional letter to the station. The station passed it on to Hugh.

Essentially, the letter writer asked how the show dared to make a hero of Hugh Herr. "And you didn't even mention Albert Dow by name," she wrote.

Hugh, stricken, read the letter over the phone to Neil Cannon. "I think I should give all the money to Mountain Rescue," he said. He had received $1,000.

"Hugh," said Cannon, "don't move. I'll call you right back." He dialed Paul Ross and explained the situation.

Ross laughed. "Mountain Rescue has plenty of money," he said. "Tell him to keep it."

Cannon called Hugh back and repeated the exchange. "That film wasn't made about the accident," he added. "It was about what you've done since then. You deserve it."

———— • ————

Hugh grew, nearing 140 pounds again. He couldn't wait to try ice climbing now that aching calves–the bane of the ice climber, who must balance on crampon points–would be a thing of the past, and his exceptional strength could take over.

NEW HAMPSHIRE   S. PETER LEWIS

In January 1984 he, Neil Cannon, and Dan McMillan headed up to North Conway. They stayed at the home of Paul Ross, a good friend of Neil's, and on the first day went to a cliff known as Frankenstein.

Hugh swam through the snow, pushing and pulling with his arms. He lunged from one tree trunk to another. Sometimes he fell and slid backward and grabbed bushes. He ripped his ski pants. But he was laughing when he arrived at the base of the ice flows.

As the three laid their ropes in ready coils in the snow, Neil teased Hugh about how much more dangerous ice climbing is than rock climbing. "Here, you lead," he said. "You've got something to prove."

But Neil led the pitch, as this was Hugh's first time on ice in two years. As Hugh easily seconded, two other climbers approached. "Hey, that's Hugh Herr up there," one said in low tones.

At the top Dan told Hugh what had been said and then pretended to be repeating his own response. He extended one arm oratorically and placed the fingertips of his other hand on his chest. "Well, *I* happen to be Dan McMillan!" he said. "I am a *lot* more famous than Huey Herr."

"So how'd it feel, Hugh?" Neil asked. "You looked really solid."

"Great," said Hugh. "I won't even have to work at it. There's no calf fatigue, and with these short crampons there's less torque to twist the prostheses away from the ice. It's everything I predicted."

The next day the three headed up to the thousand-foot face of Cannon Mountain, a remote and forbidding cliff in Franconia Notch. It is the site of one of the region's most classic ice routes, the steep and dank *Black Dike*. That route had been declared unclimbable by the great ice pioneer Yvon Chouinard, and its first ascent finally went to a seventeen-year-old no one had ever heard of, John Bouchard, who did it solo. En route, Bouchard dropped his hammer, his eyes froze shut, and a short length of rope, which he had brought to use for protection in isolated sections, jammed in a piton below him; he untied himself from it and finished the climb. His was a visionary act, and in the first few years afterward many had doubted his ascent. Hugh loved the story and had always wanted to do the route.

The cliff is preceded by a thousand feet of talus, of interlocked stones and boulders, some of which rock when weighted. Hugh crashed, pulled, and slid on his belly. It wasn't the talus but the deep snow that slowed him so much. The snow tended to pull off his legs when he tried to lift them to take steps.

At first Dan and Neil waited periodically, but soon the question hung in the air whether Hugh could get up the boulder fields at all. He was moving at a glacial pace.

"Hugh, we'll go ahead and get everything ready," Neil finally said to him.

"Sure," said Hugh. "If I can't get there in a reasonable amount of time, just start without me and I'll meet you back at the car."

Neil and Dan plowed ahead, arrived at the base of the route, uncoiled the ropes, and put on their crampons. They looked down the talus. No sign of Hugh.

Dan led the first pitch. Neil followed, trailing a rope that Hugh could tie into as soon as he arrived. Neil joined Dan at the first belay. They both looked out over the empty slopes below.

"I guess he went back to the car," said Neil, downcast.

"Aww. He really wanted to do it."

"He really tried." He looked at his watch. "I guess we have to—"

"Hey!" interrupted Dan. "Look!" From a clump of trees near the top of the slope Hugh had crawled into sight.

"It's the lizard!" Neil yelled. He and Dan broke into cheers. "Yay, lizard!" they shouted. All three knew that as soon as he reached the base of the cliff, he'd blitz the rest.

———— • ————

"It's not an advantage," said Russ Clune flatly one night that spring, sitting in the Bacchus restaurant in New Paltz. "Maybe Huey just has to see it that way. His ankles don't torque. Do you realize what a handicap that is? It's just that he makes up for it. Everything I've ever seen Hugh do is the result of phenomenal, phenomenal strength. He could have been world class."

"He *is* world class," said Neil Cannon.

14

Hugh stayed at home in Lancaster most of the winter of 1983–1984. He spent much of his time working alone on his legs, thinking and designing. By now he was well beyond the time when he had pink feet with toes. His climbing feet got smaller and smaller. He could barely walk in them; he teetered along, looking delicate, like a slightly unsteady daddy longlegs.

He wore cup-shaped plastic sockets molded to fit his stumps and held on with Velcro straps wrapped around his legs above the knees. At the bottom of the sockets were brackets into which he fit lengths of lightweight tubing.

It was two years since the accident. Though he had calmed down at the ring of a phone, he still felt clammy when the mail came.

———•———

That January Tony and Sally went to Rio de Janeiro with Russ Clune. Sally accompanied the two men at first, seeing the city and botanical gardens, swimming, and going to restaurants, but had made her plans to leave in a week. She had been to many climbing areas before, going as far away as Alaska, but though she, who had barely traveled before meeting Tony, had often enjoyed visiting those places, she had never really cared for climbing herself—or for waiting out Tony's climbing days.

During that week she and Tony took long walks on the beach and acknowledged the cracks that had appeared in their relationship. Tony urged her to try to make the marriage work, and she agreed to.

After she left, Tony and Russ climbed together, and met and climbed with the Rio locals. They managed a major new route on Sugarloaf, a cliff just above the city; it was six pitches long, 5.11-plus, and they named it *Birds of Prey*. They also did the first free ascent of a former aid route.

After his flight back to Philadelphia, Tony arrived home in Lancaster late in the evening. The house was dark as he opened the front door and dumped his pack with a satisfied "Hmpph" of breath. He shrugged off his Polarfleece jacket, walked into the kitchen, flicked on the overhead light, and opened the refrigerator door.

He stared at a plate of spaghetti covered in clear plastic wrap. Fuzzy, feathery gray mold rode up and down the small hillocks. He let out his breath shakily. It was the mold that told him.

———————— • ————————

One day that spring Hugh stretched out, sitting on a ledge below a route at Skytop in the Gunks. He did splits, forward and sideways. He ate one of his favorite snacks, blueberry yogurt with Reese's Cups crushed into it.

"Huey, you are *so* weird," said Russ Clune in horrified fascination. "Normal people wouldn't do that."

Hugh bolstered his normal attachment system by pulling a purple and orange ladies' girdle over each leg socket. Deftly, with an Allen wrench, he switched to rubber-toed feet. He looked up bright-eyed. "I'm the luckiest climber in the world," he cracked. "I get screwed before every climb."

"Hey, Huey," Russ began. "Claw wears lipstick." He was referring to the Australian climber Mike Law, whom Hugh admired. "What's the matter, you chicken? He wears perfume, too, Huey. You don't smell so sweet to me."

Russ offered him several slings. Hugh draped them over his head and neck, then looked at his hands, almost in surprise. "I'm just amazed at how strong I am. I'm just getting stronger and stronger and stronger." He squinted at the bulging rock above him. "I pity this route!"

———•———

In late spring of 1984 Hugh and Russ Clune went on a month-long road trip to California and Colorado. Hugh considered himself fortunate to be going with Russ. Not many people wanted to travel around the country for weeks at a time doing hard climbs. Russ was good-natured and entertaining. He had a van, too.

The van was a significant consideration. Traveling by car for Hugh would have meant walking to a tent site, walking around while putting up the tent, walking to take it down in the morning, then walking back to the car. That was time Hugh had to ration. But he could sleep in a van, and even store in it the bicycle he used for getting around.

These days, in planning to do the hardest climbs, Hugh no longer thought, "How will I do it?" He thought, "How will I get there? Over which trail?" Without his bicycle he would have been unable to reach most climbs.

Climbing trips involved more walking than anything else he did. But once he and Russ were at a cliff, Hugh had so much energy that he didn't quite appreciate the difficulty of what he was doing.

One day, cycling out to the road from the cliffs near Cascade Falls, Yosemite, Hugh came upon Steve Grossman. The last time they had seen each other was three years before, when they did *Astroman* and Half Dome, before the accident. Then, they had also worked on *Fish Crack*, a 5.11-plus fingertip crack. Steve had belayed Hugh for hours during a disappointing effort. Hugh had said that day, "I can't believe this is 5.11 and I'm having so much trouble."

Now Steve asked Hugh what he'd just done. *"Fish Crack,"* said Hugh. He had cruised it.

There were glitches. Hugh had trouble on certain climbs, generally the less steep routes that involved balance and smearing and palming, techniques used in the absence of large holds. In Yosemite, for a warmup, Russ led the 5.10 slab route *Freewheelin'* on Middle Cathedral Rock. Following, Hugh stalled. On this type of climb, a person's feet would be square to the rock, as much sole touching the rock as possible, heels pointing down or slightly sideways. Strangely, at one spot, as Hugh's feet moved up, his hands didn't. They stayed still. His feet tapped higher and higher in a counterclockwise direction, both pointing right until, his body crunched in the middle, the feet were at the three-o'clock position and the hands at nine. He was bent sideways, his hands and feet in a line parallel to the ground. Russ shouted with laughter and grabbed his camera. Just as he took the photo, Hugh fell, and Russ dropped the camera a hundred feet to the ground.

But overall Hugh was climbing very well. He and Russ did *Hang-dog Flyer* and *Dog's Roof*, both 5.12. Hugh's best effort in Yosemite was flashing the 5.11-plus *Bircheff-Williams* route, also on Middle Cathedral, which required very delicate footwork and difficult bridging.

He was constantly thinking about how he could improve and push to the next limit.

"As soon as you think you're good, you've lost it," he told Russ.

And he had to deal with setbacks. The uphill approach to a 5.11 route known as the *Moratorium*, from which they would connect to the 5.10 *East Buttress*, a thousand-foot route up the granite monolith El Capitan, would have been a half-hour walk for Russ. But because he kept by Hugh, it took them an hour and a half to reach the base of the climb. Hugh couldn't walk that far without pain.

They had done three pitches of the *Moratorium* and gotten another four up the *East Buttress* when Hugh, in an eerie echo of his brother Hans's words years ago, said, "I've got to go down."

"*What?*" said Russ. He had no idea there was any problem. "What's wrong?"

"I'm having trouble with my legs," Hugh said.

Two weeks before leaving Pennsylvania, he had complained of soreness, and his doctor had made an incision to remove some old stitches. Hugh had been surprised and angry that the incision had been an inch long. Now the spot was paining him.

"O.K.," said Russ. "Let's go." The two rappelled down, but their route had taken them away from the base of the *Moratorium*, where they'd left their packs. They touched down in a talus field well to one side.

"I'll go back up and get the packs," Russ said. He looped up and down in about half an hour, coming back down to where his path intersected with Hugh's. There was no sign of his friend. Russ didn't know whether Hugh was ahead of him or behind, so he hiked back to the van alone.

Two hours went by, and dusk began to creep into the valley. Russ was beginning to worry when Hugh finally crawled out of the trees. He had crawled the whole way, thrashing through bushes and over boulders. One look and Russ thought, "He's in a world of pain."

"How are you, Huey?"

"Eh. Hurts."

They drove back to the campsite. Both knew that this had been a failed test. Hugh had wanted to do the *West Face* of El Capitan, a long, hard 5.11 route, which happened to have a longer approach than the *Moratorium*. Several days later, Russ found someone else with whom he could do the route.

In Yosemite Hugh and Russ began climbing with Paul Hoskins, an Australian. The three drove together to the Needles, in the Sierras of California. But the rock faces were high in the mountains, at 11,000 feet, and the approach was three and a half miles. Hugh rode his bike up, although he had to push it around the switchbacks in the trail.

To descend in the evenings, he made thrilling rides down the talus. He would sit on the crossbar of the bike, his body tucked low, his knees out wide in the ready-to-fall position. He had to keep up a certain speed to have the momentum to get over the boulders. If he went too slowly, he would flip. It was like riding down steps, but noisier. He liked those rides – and he flipped only twice.

He actually did little climbing in the Needles. There was too much legwork involved in reaching the cliffs. He figured that he could either reach the cliffs or climb, but not both. And since he couldn't climb without getting there and didn't much want to sit alone in the parking lot, he continued to just go up.

He met a woman who, several days later, when she was just about to leave the area, told him that she had wanted to carry his pack for him. But she had been afraid that in asking she might offend him. Perhaps, too, she was swayed by the idea that if you help a person who is handicapped, he'll never become self-sufficient.

Hugh was caught between frustration and a kind of regret. "Here," he told her, "where it's several miles in, it would have helped so much for someone to carry my pack—or even me. It would make me more able to do the things I want to do."

He had his high points, too. One day, belayed by a friend named Russel Erickson, he started bridging and palming up a 5.11-plus route called *Peg Leg*. Russel Erickson steadfastly called out encouragement. Hugh kept himself together, concentrating on technique and not thinking about the sizable fall he could take.

A group of California climbers watched, agape. Until now, they had assumed that Hugh climbed well because he was simply so strong that he could pull himself up anything. "Boy, you can really use your feet, can't you?" said one after Hugh had come down to the base.

They had just been telling Russ how impressed they were. Russ was proud: "My *boy!*" he said, thumping Hugh's back. "Those people went wild, Hugh," he whispered.

Later in the trip the two had an argument. Russ was tired of doing all the dishes, especially as Hugh seemed to expect him to, expressing neither apologies nor thanks. He thought it was good for Hugh to be treated like anyone else.

As Hugh saw things, it was a long walk to the spigots, a walk that could injure his legs. He was angry, but he did the dishes. He felt he had no right to ask for special accommodations. But he wished he could have had them.

———————— • ————————

At home, Tony was taking the loss of his wife hard. Sally was now living with another man.

Tony called Sally's mother. "Was it children?" he asked. "Was that the problem? Did she want children? That's fine, I'd be into that."

"Tony," said his mother-in-law, "Sally has just grown up. She's had enough of that fantasy life with you."

He had only one talk with Sally. When he asked her why she'd left, she said, "I just can't talk about it now, Tony."

"Well, will you ever be able to talk about it, Sally?"

"I don't know, Tony. I don't know."

He was distraught and began spending too much time in bars. Hugh called him from California a few times. "Tony, analyze your past and learn from it, and then let it go," Hugh said. "Dwelling on it like this can only lead you toward self-destruction. Learn to do things to make yourself feel good. Every single constructive thing you do will make you feel better."

After one call, as he walked back to the van, he wondered about their losses. "There was the accident, and Albert. I lost my legs. So many emotions. If I had not been able to deal with it and never bounced back, and just stayed on morphine, people would have looked down on me. But I immediately started climbing again, blindly, like I wasn't even affected.

"I seem to be celebrated for my coldness," he thought. "Someone like Tony, who doesn't know what to do with all his emotion, is put down. People say, 'Tony, why can't you get over this? Get on with life?'"

———— • ————

Everywhere Russ, Paul, and Hugh went, Hugh caused a stir. People approached, asking many questions: about him, about how he climbed, about his prostheses. The normal exchange of conversation was skewed. In between Hugh's statements, his listeners were often rapt and breathless, waiting for him to say more. They smiled and shook their heads wonderingly. They came away thoughtful and thrilled, feeling as if they had been through an emotional experience themselves.

He sometimes got tired of having to tell his life story so many times to so many strangers. Yet, riding this tide of renown, he could be lazy, he could make no efforts, and people still thought he was cool. He didn't even have to try, and Sue Patenaude, an excellent Colorado climber, was attracted to him as soon as she laid eyes on him. Hugh's involvement with Sue was the most serious he had ever had.

Sue had a unique understanding about Hugh. In high school she had been a promising ski racer when she crashed and injured her knee. As a teenager, she had had to wear a knee brace—it had been hot and embarrassing, and she could hardly move in it—for years. She and

Hugh climbed together. As Neil did, she often carried him piggyback on trails to cliffs.

But she had had a boyfriend when she and Hugh met, a top climber himself, intelligent and steady-natured, who with black humor now named one of his new routes *Amputee Love*. In time she decided to stay with him. Eventually the two married. All three, rather remarkably, remained friends; in a complicated way, Hugh admired Harrison Dekker. "He's awesome," he said. But he felt the loss deeply, and it was a year before he fully realized how much he had cared for Sue.

In other ways, the romance was now back in Hugh's life. He was climbing brilliantly. The greatest climbs to him were the ones he barely made, the ones that made him sweat and work and plan and design. When he did a climb like that, he said, it felt "incredible and romantic and everlasting."

At the end of their western trip, Hugh, Russ, and Paul went to North Conway. Hugh decided to stay. John Bouchard had offered him a job making climbing equipment, such as packs and harnesses, in his and his wife's shop, called Wild Things. John was a local climber; Titoune, a Frenchwoman, had been a leading climber in Chamonix. As a team, they had tackled many demanding mountain faces. Hugh could stay in a cabin that John owned in the woods.

For Hugh it was a chance to work and climb. But he was very much afraid for both emotional and practical reasons. Could he be independent, and manage without visiting his prosthetist every week, without his parents and family to help him? Could he live alone? He wouldn't have a car. He could ride a bike around North Conway – but what if his legs were hurting? What about doing laundry, getting groceries? Still, this seemed to be one of the few jobs in the climbing industry that he could manage. He couldn't have worked retail, for example, which requires standing. Only later did he see the move in terms of a chance to resolve something with the people of the area.

Before Paul left, he and Hugh checked out the moves on *Stage Fright*, a one-pitch aid route on the same cliff tier as *Tourist Treat*.

"It'll be really good, Hugh," Paul called as he rappelled the route. He paused a quarter of the way down and locked his rappel device. "There's a really good fingerlock here," he observed. He lowered again. "It looks quite hard all the way to that last fingerlock."

He stopped again at a section where the crack closed to see whether there were any possibilities for placing protection. "You can get something in here," he said. He measured, eyeing the crack up and down, and pointed above his head. "If you fall off here, you're O.K. You probably wouldn't want to fall off any higher."

He reached the ground and gave his assessment. "It's such a good line, really hard and scary – which makes it good, because those are the ones you remember. Those are the best. I'd jump on it if I had more time here."

Russ and Paul carried Hugh's belongings from the van the eighth of a mile down the trail to the cabin. Paul would be leaving for Australia in a few weeks. Hugh hugged him. Arms at his side, Paul blushed.

The first day after Russ and Paul left, it rained. Hugh lingered awkwardly in the International Mountain Equipment shop, flipping through guidebooks and other books on climbing. His friend Elaine, working there, was concerned about him. But the next evening, when she saw him there again, he was hurrying off with several young climbers to a barbeque. Among them was Jim Surette.

Jim, fifteen, another teenaged rock climber, had grown up in North Conway, where his father published *Fly Fisherman* magazine. Jim had first met Hugh during the *Black Dike* visit in winter. He didn't think about the accident and rescue; his first thought was, "Cool! A real climber's come here."

Jim watched Hugh climb and knew he was stronger than anyone Jim had seen before. Jim asked a lot of questions. Hugh knew what was happening in other parts of the country, knew what Boulder climbers like Christian Griffith and Harrison Dekker and others around the nation were doing, things Jim had picked up only in scraps from magazines. Hugh knew that the established North Conway routes were no longer hard relative to what was happening nationally. He had a modernist's attitude and was into cragging – doing hard moves, working on hard routes for multiple days and through multiple falls. He was also excited about climbing in a way that Jim had rarely seen.

———— • ————

Hugh was having trouble walking back to his cabin at night. He'd stumble, lurch, and dive over the ruts and tree roots on the rough path.

He would arrive streaked with sweat, bitten by insects, his heart pounding with the effort. Then he would climb the ladder to his loft and sleeping bag, and try to switch his mind and body into another realm.

"Hugh," he would say to himself, "sleep."

Neil Cannon, who traveled from Hanover to climb, often stayed overnight at friends' houses. He began bringing Hugh along and letting him sleep in the back of his truck. In the morning Neil would drive into town.

"It's great," Hugh said to him cheerfully. "I go to sleep, and I wake up at the Big Pickle."

"Some people have a German shepherd in the back of the car to guard their things," said Neil. "I have a lizard." But Neil wasn't always around.

After about two weeks, John and Titoune Bouchard took Hugh into their home to live until he could find his own place. That setup, although temporary, was ideal. After working all day, Hugh could climb on the stone wall cut with handholds and footholds that the Bouchards had erected in their shop. Or he could catch a ride to the cliff.

Hugh ate with the Bouchards and went with Titoune the few miles into town to buy groceries or run errands. In the morning he had to walk only a hundred feet to work, right next door. To Hugh, the Bouchards were surrogate parents.

He stayed with them for two weeks, and they helped him find a room in a nearby boardinghouse. Then he rode his bicycle to and from work. To do household tasks, he simply crawled on his hands and knees.

Titoune accepted Hugh fully. When people questioned her about hiring Hugh Herr, she said firmly, "He's suffered enough." She liked him.

Yet even as Hugh was absorbed into daily North Conway life, he felt that he was always on probation, and that some people thought he couldn't understand their pain. Once, in reaction to a controversial mountaineering decision, he said, "Oh, that was stupid." The words had just slipped out. The room immediately fell quiet, and he saw that in the eyes of the others, he had no normal right to make judgments. In ensuing months and years, he was to voice no others. It sometimes seemed as if people were waiting for him to make a mistake. But no one – in stores, in restaurants, at the cliffs – ever said anything harsh to him. Most people were pleasant to his face. Even some who had seemed to avoid him were now civil.

One day when a man left the International Mountain Equipment shop, a young woman behind the counter jerked her thumb at his receding back and remarked to her coworker, Elaine Watkins, "He's a real Huey Hater."

Said Elaine, "Who is he? Is he a climber?"

"Not really. I think he's just trying to jump on a bandwagon." She hesitated, then continued. "I heard that at a bar the other night he said, 'When I die, I want this written on my stone: Hugh Herr, I'll never forgive you.'"

———— • ————

A young climber from Australia who had lost a leg when hit by a drunk motorcyclist called Hugh once from the Gunks to say she might visit. Then one evening around eight or nine she phoned Wild Things; she had just arrived in town. Titoune picked her up at the bus station and drove her to Hugh's boardinghouse. As it was late, there wasn't much time to talk. Hugh, feeling awkward, helped set Pam up on the floor of his small room.

The next day Pam wanted advice, but Hugh felt he couldn't give much: her problem was completely different from his. She had lost her leg much higher – she had no knee – and had different movements, different angles. She used an artificial leg for walking, and a peg for climbing. Hugh tried to fit her with one of his feet, but he could see it wouldn't work. When the two went climbing together, Hugh's much greater range of motion became obvious. It took Pam a long time just to get up the hill to the base of Cathedral Ledge. Nevertheless, she was ambitious and talked about climbing Mount McKinley.

He took her up a popular 5.6, *Refuse*. At the top, the two decided to go back down the cliff rather than walk down the road to the parking lot. As they had only one rope, rather than the two that would have made the rappel simple, Hugh decided simply to lower Pam off, then down-climb. He would essentially be soloing, but at this easy grade, he didn't mind.

LANCASTER COUNTY, PENNSYLVANIA   ANTHONY HERR

Marc Chauvin, an International Mountain Equipment climbing school instructor, was with a client when Pam lowered into sight. Chauvin's client turned to him and said quietly, "Now I've seen everything."

Chauvin smiled. "No, you haven't." He knew whom she was with.

"O.K.!" Pam shouted up to Hugh from a ledge. "I'm safe."

The man's jaw slacked as Hugh tiptoed down backward. Sunlight glinted off his lightweight aluminum tubes. "Excuse me," said Hugh as he passed close by.

———— • ————

Hugh teamed up often with Jim Surette. Jim never asked him about the accident; they just climbed.

Jim began picking up on Hugh's personality: the single-mindedness, the newly returned confidence, the delight in shocking people with outlandish clothes. He took to wearing Hugh's "Herr Pants." Hugh even began topping his ensembles off, rock-and-roll-singer style, with eyeliner and nail polish. At the time he was frequently painting his hands with benzoyl peroxide as a base, and winding adhesive tape over that to help prevent abrasion and tendon injury. He and Jim thought the nail polish on the stained brown fingers looked very, very cool. Jim began dyeing his gymnast's chalk with a few drops of food coloring. Then both the tape on his hands and his skin turned green.

When Hugh first showed up, Jim had just been starting to get good, by area standards, at climbing. After the two began climbing together, Jim got much better. He learned from Hugh to raise his ambitions, to focus. Joined by Neil Cannon, they set their sights on putting up ever-harder routes in New Hampshire.

Jim, too, began working at Wild Things. Then the two were all the more able to make plans to climb in their time off.

Though generally quiet around others, they wisecracked continually to each other. While leading, belayed by Hugh, Jim might tease, "You could have trouble here. These moves aren't as easy as I'm making them look." There was, in fact, no rivalry between them. Hugh, the stronger climber, encouraged Jim, made him feel good about his climbing and his potential, gave him shots of confidence.

Hugh began experimenting with legs of different lengths. He realized that adjusting his leg length made no difference to his foot "feel." His phantom awareness extended from his ankle to the bottom of his foot. It seemed to have nothing to do with the connecting artificial leg.

He tried short legs, long legs, more crack feet, more kinds of rubber. Whenever he got new feet in the mail, he would be delighted. He would talk about how he might alter them, where he might shave or chop parts off, or grind them down. The whole prospect of designing legs and feet to fit particular rock-climbing problems was so exciting to Jim that he sometimes startled himself by almost wishing he didn't have legs.

Hugh was ever less concerned about people's reactions to his amputations. One time when his legs were bothering him, he crawled into a Hardees and gave his order from the floor. He thought that was hilarious.

———•———

One day in mid-August Neil and Jim Surette went up a long route, *Lights in the Forest,* in hopes of free-climbing its two aid pitches. They succeeded on the first, grading the hard move over the roof at 5.11-plus. They didn't have time to finish the project that day and brought Hugh and Elaine Watkins along when they returned.

Jim and Neil climbed the overhang quickly. Then Hugh and Elaine took turns trying and falling, swinging off the roof, laughing, fighting over handholds in the rock as they unweighted the rope while Jim, above, switched to belay one and then the other.

Elaine, rocking onto a flexed foot, finally made it over the roof, wondering how Hugh would ever manage the move. But he, too, succeeded on his next try.

"How did you ever do that?" she asked.

"This heinous pinch," he replied breathlessly. The three stared at him and then roared with laughter, barely believing that he had been able to pull himself over a roof using such a strenuous hold. A climber can grab such a hold only with straight fingers and thumb, rather than curling his hand around it. They'd never even noticed the pinch.

Jim went up to investigate the last pitch but was only able to report that it would "definitely go" before lowering down, thwarted by descending darkness. The four rappelled together, elated.

But at the bottom, Hugh and Elaine came to an awkward moment. Elaine had been trying to help Hugh pick up work as a climbing instructor, and the two were to jointly teach a class the next day. "So, see you tomorrow morning?" she asked.

"Umm . . . I might want to come back with these guys," he said, "and do that route."

She was silent. She realized that his motivation was the idea of having his name on the first-ascent report. That in itself was not unusual – most climbers were driven to do first ascents. But she was angry that he would skip the first day on a new job for publicity's sake.

"Do you think that would be bad, not to come?"

"Yes," she said tightly.

The next day Hugh met the class at the appointed hour. He taught climbing only a few times, however. It just wasn't steady work. One day when he was leading a client up to Cathedral, a leg fell off and went cartwheeling down the hill. It scooped and flung dirt, while bits of glued leather flew out and scattered. The client was stricken until he saw the leg's owner laughing.

———— • ————

Hugh and Neil began an effort to do the first free ascent of a former aid line, *Fortitude*. The first day, Neil led up the first section, a relatively easy offwidth crack of 5.8. As Hugh seconded, Neil, who was leaning back on a ledge in the sun, said, "Hugh, how are you in offwidths?"

Below, Hugh gasped. "Take me!" It was climbers' jargon for "Catch me, I'm falling."

Even as Neil said, "What?" the rope pulled taut and jerked him across the ledge. He peered over the side to see Hugh looking up, swinging on the rope, clutching it in both hands. As their moment of terror passed, they both laughed until their faces hurt.

They took turns trying steep hard moves leading to a difficult mantel onto a sloping ledge. They had to fight to keep the steep wall from pushing them off backward. After several days of taking repeated fifteen-foot falls onto a large Stopper slotted into a crack on the face below, they were compelled to give *Fortitude* a rest while Neil returned to graduate school. They agreed that if everything was right and the leader was daring, they could do it.

Hugh turned to *Tourist Treat*. That prize had repelled many strong climbers. Though Hugh worked and worked on the route, he could neither fit his foot into a high pod at the crux section nor turn it sideways. When he tried to use that hold, his body was forced outward. Yet he was getting his head up high enough that he could see into the better crack above, so he gave up temporarily on the foot and, frustrated, started jumping for the crack, trying to hit it on the fly.

He tried climbing *Tourist Treat* in shorter legs than he'd ever used. They affected his personality; he got silly when he was small. "Hey, this is great," he'd giggle, flapping his arms like a seal. "So this is how Lynnie does it," he said, referring to five-foot-one Lynn Hill. Then, before going out to dinner at a restaurant in town, he might change into long shanks and become six feet fall. With the height he grew serious, dignified, and mature. Sometimes, out at the cliffs, he was even eight feet tall. Unable to flex his ankles, Hugh simply increased his reach by increasing his leg length.

He settled down to being about six feet tall. "I think this is what I would have been," he explained.

He made a special shank for *Tourist Treat*, a minute red leg, which he hoped to worm into the pod so that he could squat on it without having his body pushed outward. But when he tried to use it on the route, he found he could barely do the 5.11 moves to reach the crux.

In late August, Lynn Hill came to town with Russ Raffa. She got on *Tourist Treat* and, after one fall, did the route. Hugh and Russ took turns trying to follow her, and although Russ finally clawed to the top, Hugh didn't manage it.

"Have you heard the news?" people were asking in the climbing shops the next morning. "Lynn Hill did *Tourist Treat!*"

The glory and chance for greater fame stolen, Hugh burned with hurt pride and frustration. He had put so much time and thought into the route. The experience did lead to a positive, confidence-enhancing result, however. In the Big Pickle the day after Hill's ascent, as Neil began talking about *Fortitude,* Hugh said, "This is it. I realize the problem. I've been holding back, letting myself fall. If I would just release and let go, I'd make it."

That day he charged up the route. He set the customary Stopper for protection and blasted up to the hard mantel. Neil, holding the rope, saw something that made his stomach weak. The Stopper usually wedged itself in tight during the course of the first fall or two. Today it hadn't, and when the rope lifted up after Hugh, the loose Stopper rose up out of the crack and slid down to Neil.

Hugh, midmantel, was now in a position to fall eighty feet to the ground. Neil said nothing, fearing that to break Hugh's concentration would make him fall.

Hugh knew he was risking a substantial fall, although he didn't dream just how long. But he also knew his body, and he knew he was solid. He felt that he was soloing, and that falling could not have any part in his plans. He pulled the mantel off and cruised to the belay.

Fortitude was a milestone for Hugh: he once again demonstrated the boldness that had enabled him to succeed on *Super Crack.* But it was not an unconsidered boldness, it was not recklessness. It was very carefully planned.

When Neil told him about the pulled Stopper, Hugh just shrugged his shoulders. "I wasn't going to fall anyway," he said.

———— • ————

Over the summer Hugh became known to the locals. Brenda Wilcox, whose husband, Rick, owned International Mountain Equipment, had been taken aback when she first saw Hugh in her husband's store. But she took her cue from Rick, who was president of Mountain Rescue (he had been out of the country during the Herr-Batzer accident), and from her own instincts. "You get to know Hugh," she said, "and he's real, and he's just so cute, you can't help but like him."

After he had been in North Conway for several months, Hugh joined a volleyball league, which played in the lecture hall right across the street from International Mountain Equipment. He always tried to play hard, but it was painful. One night the pain hit him so badly that he sat straight down on the floor. For a moment he couldn't get up.

Everyone was asking, "Are you all right?"

Hugh looked up at Michael Hartrich, the man who'd been caught in the avalanche with Albert Dow, and saw his face change. It wasn't that Hartrich had ever had a hard attitude toward Hugh. But that night Hartrich took a special interest; he wanted to talk to him. After the game he invited Hugh to his house. Hugh thought that Michael was crusty on the outside, nice on the inside; he liked that.

Steve Larson, another volunteer who had been up Odell's during the rescue, was gracious from the start. Once, in the parking lot at Cathedral Ledge, Hugh asked about a new route Steve had just done. They chatted for a long time and the following weekend went climbing together. But on that day one of Hugh's legs broke; the threads in a bolt were stripped.

"I have to cut new threads in the hole," Hugh said. "I need a tap."

"I know someone who has one," said Steve. "Let me call him." He drove Hugh into town, made the call, and then ran Hugh out to the friend's house, where they fixed the problem.

Kurt Winkler was one of the people who didn't have to say anything. His friendly attitude told Hugh he was accepted.

Henry Barber approached Hugh at a party that summer. His wife, Jill, watched apprehensively. Henry was always forthright with people, and she never knew what he might pop off with. "I just want to tell you," Barber said to Hugh, "that I have a good feeling about you, a really good feeling." He laughed his usual loud, uninhibited yelp, tipped his beer, and moved on to entertain someone else.

Hugh these days felt strong; he felt his potential was back; he felt accepted in the community. He was contented and excited about life. He said to a New Hampshire friend, Peter Lewis, "God picked the right person for this to happen to."

————— ● —————

One fall day Hugh said, "I hurt my elbow. It's really bad, Elaine. Really." He shook his head slowly, mouth pressed downward in disgust.

"Every time you hurt yourself, it's always because you're showing off," Elaine told him. "You were doing one-arm pull-ups for Brenda, Titoune, and Karin. Brenda told me."

"It wasn't just that," said Hugh. He had been overtraining, and also making many repetitive motions as he cut and sewed at work. Such tendinitis later became common among climbers, but at the time Hugh had little information from which to make predictions about recovering. In ensuing weeks he became more depressed than he had been after the accident. Climbers' overuse injuries are serious and often chronic, and this was the first time Hugh believed he might not ever be able to climb well again. Even after the accident, he'd had faith, hope, and power, and had never let go. He had been more ashamed and furious than depressed. But now he found himself having to relinquish many of his ambitions.

It pleased him when his picture – stretching and straining on *Tourist Treat*, shirtless and muscular – appeared on the cover of *Climbing* magazine, but it also made him wistful.

———————— • ————————

Two months later, in winter, Hugh lay sleeping on a couch by the stove in the rental house he shared with a friend and co-worker, Randy Ratliff, on West Side Road. As the stove was the only source of heat, on cold nights Hugh often slept on the couch rather than in his own back room. Occasionally Jim Surette stayed over and slept on the couch opposite.

In a dream, Hugh looked down, detached, on himself and Jim on their couches. He saw himself suddenly sit up and his eyes, robotlike, spring open. With jerky, mechanical movements, the dream-Hugh turned toward his feet. He threw the covers back, as if expecting something. And he had perfect legs. He turned and looked at Jim.

Jim sat up, moving in the same disjointed way, and turned his head first this way, then that. He threw his own covers off. The two stared at Jim's legs. They were bloated and gangrenous, the mummified skin peeling, the jaundiced ankle bone showing. Both boys gasped.

Instantly, tinnily, Hugh said, "Jimmy, it's O.K. It's only a dream." He knew, in his sleep, that it was wrong for him to have legs, and Jim not to.

He woke up. It was the first dream in which he was aware of the amputations. His mind had finally accepted the reality. He was twenty.

———•———

In spring Hugh rented a room in a house on Seavey Street in town. One day a big man, well over six feet tall, hove into his doorway.

"Could you turn your TV down?" he asked. "I'm in the next room." Then he saw that Hugh, lying in bed with his artificial legs propped against the wall, had no feet.

"What happened?" he asked. Then, "Oh, you're the guy from Mount Washington."

Lying there without his legs, Hugh felt his vulnerability wash over him. "Uh-oh," he thought. But the man leaned against the wall and assumed a conversational manner.

"You don't still feel guilty about Albert Dow, do you?" he said.

"Yes."

"Well, Albert used to talk about how noble it would be to save someone's life. He would have been willing to give his life. Besides, from the type of person he was, I think he'd be the last one to want you to feel this way."

———•———

Hugh had been resting his elbow and doing physical therapy all winter. He was ready to climb again. In March 1985 he and Jim did a hard new route, a 5.12-minus they named *The Breeze*, but he knew he wanted something else. He had been getting less and less creative. For the first time he had mixed feelings about climbing.

Climbing at his level *and* dealing with the physical problems of being mobile was too much. It was the hardest thing he had ever done. "You have to be young," he thought. "I can't always do both."

He got a book, Area Publishing's *Preparation for the S.A.T.*, and began studying to take the college entrance exams. He studied often and hard.

15

There was one climb Hugh still wanted to do: *Stage Fright*. He had been on it. It would probably be solid 5.12 or 5.12-plus. What made the route exceptionally difficult was the lack of cracks deep enough for a climber to place protection. Rappelling down to the crux and drilling a bolt to clip into would have created a thunderhead in the New Hampshire climbing community, whose ethic dictated climbing routes and placing protection from the ground up. Drilling bolts on rappel would also have made the route into yet another elevated boulder problem, Hugh reasoned, something one could fall off thoughtlessly and indefinitely, something that didn't require commitment.

"Mostly," as he told Neil Cannon, "bolting it would be an invitation for many youths to have a siege party." He laughed mischievously. "I'm hiding behind ethics to protect myself from competition."

He began working on the route, trying all of the latest gear trinkets available for protection. John Bouchard rappelled the route. "Hugh," he said, "I've seen too many deaths in my climbing career. I do not want to belay you." To a co-worker, he said that he'd never seen anything like it.

Jim Surette, however, willingly belayed Hugh day after day on the route. Hugh talked a few others into belaying turns as well. He even tried to sweeten the request by providing his belayers with lawn chairs and music, rock-and-roll that issued from a boom box.

All told, Hugh put about twenty days into the route, working out the various 5.12 sequences that led to the still more difficult crux. The climbing was ill-suited to his feet. For someone else the crux move would involve rocking onto a foot. As Hugh couldn't rock, his weight was thrown to the side until he was almost laybacking off a hold at his ankle. This crux was a blank section topped by a pocket in the crack above. Because Hugh's body was pushed sideways, he could not make a static reach to that pocket. It would have to be a lunge—the most dynamic, committing move in a climber's repertoire.

For this route, he synthesized all of his analytical skills. He thought through the moves and the belay system. He climbed tied into two light, nine-millimeter ropes, clipping each into some small but well-set brass R.P.s. He would climb until the R.P.s were about eight feet below his waist. Then he would place a camming device called a Slider Nut into an old piton hole. That was the hardest part of his engineering plan. Because of Hugh's body position, he wouldn't be able to see the placement well and would have to make it by feel. If he fell from above the Slider and it pulled out, he could possibly hit the ground twenty-five feet below.

"Jim," he said one day, "I could die up here."

But he reasoned that if he used two ropes—one threaded through the Slider, the other passing through the more secure nuts below it— his belayer should be able to take in slack fast with the second rope as Hugh fell. Instead of thinking, "You could hit the deck," Hugh thought, "You have two safety systems. The Slider would have to fail *and* the belay system would have to fail. That's not likely." And neither system would be necessary at all unless he fell hard.

He took small, experimental falls on the Slider, which never popped. Then, trying to work his way a little higher on the climb's moves, he took some slightly more serious ones.

He and Jim always used two ropes, but they also worked out a further refinement. Belaying, Jim stood on a narrow grass ledge just above a low-angled slab that was the finishing section of a popular 5.6

named *Thin Air*. As Hugh began risking the more sizable falls on the Slider, Jim would tie himself with a six-foot length of rope to a tree on the ledge and prepare to jump off onto the slab below. He could take a lot of slack out of the rope system that way, in case the Slider popped with Hugh well above it.

At first, as he tried *Stage Fright* with normal-length legs, Hugh found he could not come close to a chance at the crux moves. So he increased his leg length. "It's the ultimate testpiece," he told his friend Peter Lewis, a photographer who took pictures of him on the climb, "because I have to change my body to do it."

More and more, however, he was terribly afraid of injuring himself on the climb. Worse still, inherent in the attempt lay the potential to fail again in New Hampshire.

Even if no one had ever been against him, even if it weren't for Albert, he would have been fighting this fear. Hugh pictured himself falling, injured, in the hospital, paralyzed, written up in the press, with people saying, "God, look what he's done now," with people hating him and calling him reckless.

The death of Albert and his own loss elevated his fight to a struggle against his own horror. Lying in bed now, staring up, he felt the atrocity of the past incident and knew he could relive it all, easily. With one fall he could be there again. And this time, the second time, it would be worse.

The route was such an emotional struggle that he decided it would be his last at this level of physical and psychological danger. "I can't do this anymore," he thought. Taking the risks was too exhausting; the route would test every fiber of his mental strength. Yet it could be his tribute to himself, a statement to himself that he could overcome.

After only the first day's attempt, sitting to take off his climbing feet, he had known it. He'd said, "I'm never going to do anything like this again." Hugh questioned himself endlessly, often thinking of quitting. But he wanted to leave New Hampshire – and he couldn't until he did the route. *Stage Fright* became Hugh's great obsession. He wanted to do it and end it.

In practical terms, he knew this kind of route was his forte: a steep, unprotected lead that required placing wired nuts on a blank wall. It

Hugh Herr, eleven, wrote a ten-page story about climbing, based on his summer trip with his father and brothers to Mount Rainier. They had bivouacked at ten thousand feet in Camp Muir, and then made the final ascent.

"My dad was tired and he dragged on the rope. I was going to tell him to quit it but when I opened my mouth he stuck a piece of chocolate in my mouth. I didn't say a word and then we went on. We rested again and the same thing happened except he slapped a piece of baloney in my hand. . . .

"At the summit the snow went up a little. I stood on it, and I said to myself, 'I am really at the top.'"

was what he'd been doing in the Shawangunks. To do something that difficult and dangerous would be a testament; he believed it was a vision.

Hugh was so consumed by the climb that while waiting for Jim to belay him at four, when school was out, he would lie in bed, concentrating on the moves, psyching himself, preparing himself. To Jim and Neil it seemed that he could talk about nothing but the route and the sequence of moves.

"Oh, shut up about that," Jim would say.

Neil would tease him. "Hey, Huey," he'd ask, "what's the sequence for *Stage Fright*?"

At night Hugh dreamed of the route, seeing every move and piece of protection clearly. "Please, little Slider, be good," he whispered as he placed it. He lunged above it, and then he was falling. The dream showed him a close-up view of the Slider bursting from the rock. Then he crashed to the ground amid the shards of his artificial legs.

His body jerked and he woke up, head hurting, the climbing sequences still in his mind. They faded as he realized he had been dreaming. But then they came back.

———— • ————

On July 20, Hugh recruited Dave Rose to belay him. Dave was older than Jim, and Hugh was reluctant to ask him to be jumping off ledges, so he also asked Steve Larson to belay on the second rope. Steve was to manage the rope attached to the Slider. If Hugh fell onto the Slider, Steve would let out a little bit of slack, to make the fall more dynamic and lessen the shock-load on the Slider. Dave, on the other hand, was ready to reel in two armloads of the backup rope, clipped into the tiny but better-placed R.P.s. Both belayers had the ropes through Sticht plate friction devices.

By now Hugh had been doing the hard moves up to the crux so quickly and easily that everyone knew it was only a matter of time before he would finish the route. As he put on his climbing feet and the gear sling containing the nuts he'd need if he made the lunge, all knew this could be the day. There was really nothing left for Hugh to do except commit.

Dave was worried. Hugh had taken only short falls so far on the Slider nut. He knew Hugh to be the ultimate rock engineer – if anyone could make that Slider stick, it was Hugh. But Dave also recalled that Hugh had so far always stood on tiny edges, his body in close to the rock. Whenever he had fallen, his feet had always skittered down the surface of the rock. The Slider had never taken an outward pull – or a hard fall.

Hugh wasn't thinking any of that. He had made all his calculations. Now it was just a matter of clearing his mind and doing what he knew he had to do.

Twenty feet up the seam, Hugh pressed his hips against the rock face and with his right hand hauled on a flat-edged sidepull. His left groped above in the shallow seam. His whole body teetered, wanting to swing off the wall like a barn door. He placed one foot on a sloping mound in the wall, quietly unclipped the Slider nut, and stuffed it into the crack at chest-height. The move was awkward and he had to balance carefully, but he had a good foothold. He tugged on the Slider, testing it.

His leg began to shake, the vibrations creeping down his shank. It was time for the lunge to a pocket three and a half feet above him. He must let go of the rock, let go of fear.

Hugh blocked his emotions. Somewhere right near him, but held just at bay, was the nightmare to be relived. But in his mind were only the moves and a deep-rooted drive to think positively, to keep himself alive.

His right foot was on the little ramp, his right hand on the little sidepull. He would have to push off and let go with both his left foot and his right hand.

He pulled his body down, once, in the direction of his weighted left foot. His eyes saw nothing but the pocket. He lunged, left foot in the air, right still pasted on. He hit the pocket perfectly.

He stuffed three fingers into it and reached for the crack above, slotting his fingers partway in. The edges of the crack were sharp, and in the back it widened. It felt hollow. He locked his fingers into the tapering outer edges of the crack. Now the Slider was at his feet; he had never been so high above it.

There was more to go. He didn't feel his own fear. The only fear he noticed was that of the belayers fidgeting far below. He saw a young man lying in the snow, thinking not of his sorrow but of his parents'.

Tiring, he threw in a #4 R.P.–the size of a pencil eraser–that went in only sideways, on its edges. Dave and Steve didn't realize it wasn't good. They were shouting, "Good job, Huey! Nice going!" Then they suddenly fell silent as they saw him shaking. He pulled his body upward another foot and banged in a better nut. The belayers shouted again. Hugh put in one more nut and moved on.

He had a sense that his arms were pulling the rock down, that his body was delivering him wherever his eyes pointed.

Now his fingers were plugging deep into the crack.

Now he was at the top, no longer spent, wild.

"Got youuuuuu *Stage Fright!*"

The nightmare hadn't happened. He was in a frontier, in a place where no one had been, in a magic instant.

———— • ————

The elation lasted a long, long time, for days after Hugh packed his belongings, for days after he reached home in Lancaster. He had opened a new door in pushing to the level he'd attained for *Stage Fright*. He could still hear Dave saying that, all factors taken into account, this could be the hardest climb in the country. For him the crux had probably been 5.13.

Accolades came: an account by Peter Lewis in *Climbing*, a poster made from one of Peter's shots of Hugh on the route, a description of the climb in Ed Webster's area guidebook as a "bold statement of dedication and excellence by Hugh Herr."

But on the day after he did *Stage Fright*, Hugh locked himself in his room on Seavey Street and cried for a whole day. He was neither happy nor sad; he exploded, not knowing quite why, in exhaustion and release.

In completing *Stage Fright*, he had been reliving his emotions in reverse, leaving the hospital and going back into the Great Gulf, to the top of the mountain, to Odell's.

He realized he didn't have to go through that again. It was as if he had reached the top of Odell's and turned around and walked down.

16

A few days after he finished *Stage Fright*, Hugh went back to Pennsylvania and enrolled in college at Millersville University. He was a little nervous about how he'd manage in college. "You know how to work," he coached himself, "and you know you have the willpower."

Don Eidam, assistant chairman of the department of computer science and Hugh's academic adviser, met the young man the first day of school, at orientation. He knew about Hugh from old news accounts. With a bit of prejudice, he wondered whether Hugh would be back on campus the next year. He figured that as a climber and farm boy, Hugh was probably not intellectually committed. Don had spent a few years in southern Lancaster County, a mile from Hugh's house. He referred to the area as Appalachia.

But Hugh seemed unexpectedly mature and intent. He came in talking about taking a 100-level math course, and although he lacked the normal college-preparatory curriculum record from high school (he had taken vocational courses instead), Don persuaded him to sign up for a 110-level trigonometry class.

As school began, Hugh found himself happy. The system seemed beautifully simple: be here at eight, here are some problems, solve them. The institution, he felt, took care of him, gave him a supporting framework. It had gotten so taxing for him to be creative under his own motivation.

Here, too, Hugh was unknown. Although he had enjoyed the press he'd received, a sudden pleasure in his anonymity made him realize that he was tired of fame. Climbers whom he had never met knew all about him and often had already decided whether to like him or not; with his classmates, however, he was simply another student.

Having done virtually no homework in high school, Hugh now took to his studies. He tape-recorded lectures, he studied for tests by having his mother give him home quizzes, he immersed himself in his books. If anything, he had too much discipline.

He found himself applying one of his favorite techniques, that of reducing a problem to its abstract, its essence. In his math classes, and later in physics, he would find himself very effective at narrowing a large amount of information into what was important to solving the problem.

Discovering that he was especially good at mathematical problems, Hugh wondered whether he had developed an intelligence for math through climbing. He began to consider whether he had been obsessed not so much with climbing as with its way of thinking. Like climbing, math seemed to be all sequences, and all will.

Gradually, Hugh came to be reminded of himself as a high school student: serious and withdrawn, and not always very pleasant. Now, before an exam, he withdrew in the same way. During a test he concentrated so hard that he never looked up from his desk. That delighted him.

"Before an exam," he told his friend Elaine Watkins on the phone, "you're sitting there waiting to get your paper, and you feel that tension like you're about to get on *Super Crack*, like, I hate this. As soon as it's over, you love it."

In extreme climbing Hugh had detached himself from his mind, from his doubts and judgments. In college he would forget about his body. He would find himself just sitting for days, reading; he sometimes had the feeling that he was a disembodied mind.

It was summer, and the Herr family was in Alaska, driving to a trailhead. Hugh was carsick.

As the children put on their sweaters and packs, Martha Herr asked Hugh whether he felt well enough to go.

"Yes!" said Hugh.

He marched along, white as chalk. "You don't have to keep going," Martha said. "Would you like to stop?"

"No!" said Hugh.

Martha didn't ask again.

Studying math, Hugh found his thinking much less disjointed than it had ever been. He could focus better than ever before. He was reminded of the rushes of happiness he had had when climbing as a teenager. School was as new and exciting a passion as that had been.

———— • ————

His first A, on a psychology exam, was followed by others in English composition, trigonometry, and music history. At the end of the first semester, when Don Eidam saw Hugh's grades, he was amazed: straight As.

One night when Hugh got together with his old classmate Bob Mullins for beers at the Harmony Inn, Hugh spoke of how happy he was to be in college, and what kind of grades he'd been getting. He told Bob, who had always urged him to go to school, "I have you to thank for this."

When Hugh got up to go to the bathroom that evening, a club bouncer went after him. "You've had too much to drink," he said. "You're going to have to leave."

Hugh, who never drank much, asked, "What are you talking about?"

"Look at the way you're walking."

Hugh thought often about Tony, who had moved to Colorado. He missed his older brother. "If Tony were here at this bar now," he said to Bob, "everyone would be here. Everyone for blocks around would have heard he was here."

As Hugh pulled 4.0 grade-point averages his second and then third semesters, Don Eidam thought, "This is no accident." He began teasing Hugh. "You better not get a B," he said. "If you get a B, I'm going to disown you and never write a recommendation for you."

Hugh would look through the college catalogue, point at a course, and say, "I'd like to take this."

"No, it's too easy for you," Eidam would counter.

They would talk for hours. Eidam liked the fact that Hugh struggled with the world, did not accept it at face value but thought more deeply than most students. Hugh also seemed natural and unaffected by the publicity Eidam knew he had received. He felt he could talk soul-to-soul with this young man. There were not many people he would have said that about.

Hugh was groping, it seemed, trying to know what to do with the rest of his life. Eidam began by steering him into computer science; although Hugh eventually switched to a physics major and was assigned a new adviser, it was Eidam who pointed him toward graduate school.

For his part, for a long time Hugh related to his professors better than to his classmates. He didn't get involved socially with the other students. He liked being anonymous, at least at school. Having always had older people–Tony's friends and climbing partners–as friends, he also felt more drawn to his professors. He had difficulty relating to students his own age.

———— • ————

It was just after his freshman year began in 1985 that Hugh first went to see Barry Gosthnian, a certified prosthetist and orthotist, in Mechanicsburg, Pennsylvania. Jeff Batzer, Hugh's Mount Washington partner and Gosthnian's patient through the York Hospital Amputee Clinic, had steered Hugh toward him. Until now, Hugh had been working with prosthetists in Philadelphia and Florida. He was having knee-cap and tendon problems. He thought they probably resulted from all the bicycle riding he had done in North Conway.

Active amputees, he knew, can eventually lose almost all mobility because of such disorders. With every step a below-knee amputee takes, his knee is subjected to greater stress than normally occurs in a biological limb. His artificial foot and shank offer little dampening, and his tendons and ligaments face the consequences.

Hugh's frequent stump-skin problems, such as abscesses and pressure cysts, now seemed trivial–because skin heals. Sometimes his joint pains and aches kept him awake at night.

It was difficult for doctors to tell him what was wrong; the problems were too subtle. As one doctor put it, "It's not like the cartilage is popping out."

Hugh told Barry Gosthnian about the pain and brought him magazine articles and photos of climbing to help explain what he sought.

"I want to be light," he said.

"O.K.," said Gosthnian. "Let's see what we can do."

He led Hugh into his lab at Orthotic and Prosthetic Specialties. Country music floated in from the radio. On the workbench were screwdrivers and a vise, a ball-peen hammer, a mallet, pin punches, rulers, screws, and a plumb bob. Buckets of plaster sat beside the workbench, and trowels and tongue depressors rested on tables. On the wall hung scissors and pliers of every size. A large jar of Vaseline, a can of Play-Doh, and a lineup of instant glues and epoxy sat on shelves. In one corner was a sink; next to a stove was a drill press. Against another wall were a bench grinder, a table saw, and an air compressor.

From the start, the two weighed every component and shaved every ounce. Instead of metal ankle joints, for example, they used plastics; on one memorable day, they knocked five and a half ounces off an ankle. They made leg sockets of acrylic and carbon composites. They reinforced the tops of Hugh's climbing feet with carbon. When they worked together, they would shove a pad and pencil back and forth, diagramming and drawing in arrows for forces. Soon Hugh was one of the very few patients whom Gosthnian would leave alone in his lab.

———— • ————

Although he had not expected to stop altogether, Hugh didn't climb during the academic year. He didn't like the idea of trying to do two things; he felt as if he would be out of control. He wouldn't be able to do both as well as he would want to.

On the phone he told Neil Cannon, who had moved to Boulder to climb more, "I don't need climbing anymore."

"Hugh," said Neil, "I think your legs introduce tension into your life. I don't get that unless I climb. I need to do physical things or I go crazy."

"I'm on the edge every day," Hugh agreed. "Sometimes I am so pathetic, I can't even do the normal day-to-day survival routine, like get my laundry done, because my legs hurt too much to walk."

He also stopped dressing wildly. The flamboyance took too much work. Besides, college was so fulfilling that he didn't need to entertain himself with clothes.

———— • ————

While Barry Gosthnian worked on Hugh's legs, Hugh was always hammering at him, asking "Is there a different kind of socket that would let me walk with less pain?"

One day he asked, "Barry, if you had all the money and time in the world, what would you design?"

"You know, I've had this idea for about ten years," Barry replied. "But whenever I tell anyone about it, they laugh their heads off.

"It's an idea for cushioning a socket with hydraulics, based on the same principle as an aircraft landing on shock struts." Gosthnian had worked as an Air Force mechanic in Vietnam. He explained to Hugh that this socket would contain a bladder whose hydraulic pressure could be varied.

The two talked about the idea, and in May 1986, Gosthnian taught the young man a crash-course in anatomy. Hugh supplemented it by buying *Gray's Anatomy*. Then they got down to work.

17

The summer he was twenty-two, after his first year at Millersville University, Hugh went to Oregon and Washington on a climbing trip. His friends Mike and Nancy Jimmerson picked him up at the airport in Portland. Mike had just taken his bar exam, and he and his wife were embarking on a two-month climbing tour.

Their first stop was Smith Rocks, several hours east, near the tiny town of Terrebonne. The three were buying ice cream at a roadside stand after a day on the cliffs when Hugh noticed a group of teenage girls giggling uncontrollably as they looked toward the counter.

He tensed. "Mike," he whispered. "Mike, those girls are laughing at me!"

Mike turned and suddenly burst out laughing. His unwashed hair was sticking straight up on his head; he was wearing a dangling earring, multicolored Lycra tights, and a pink scoop-neck top. "Huey, they're not laughing at you," he said. "They're laughing at *me!*"

In Oregon, Hugh watched the news each night to track the progress of Giles Thompson, a sixteen-year-old who had lost his lower legs after being frostbitten in a blizzard on Mount Hood in May. Giles was the main reason he had wanted to come to Oregon.

The storm had killed nine of Giles's classmates and teachers. Hugh phoned the hospital for permission to visit Giles but had to wait for several days, until the boy's condition stabilized.

Hours before starting out for the hospital, he began his preparations. He had to look perfect that day: his hair, his clothes, his technology. No pipes or screws could be showing, and he needed to be wearing human-looking prostheses. Someone who has just suffered an amputation, he knew, would be anxious about physical appearance and sex appeal. Hugh abandoned his climbing garb that day and pulled on long pants and a royal blue sweater.

When he entered Giles's room, he walked with his most normal, careful, considered gait. He told Giles that he'd lost his lower legs in a similar accident four and a half years before. "I've been climbing in the area this week," he said casually, "so I thought I'd stop by and see you."

He looked around the room and over at the boy. He hadn't thought this would affect him, but it did, profoundly. Giles was exactly, uncannily, as Hugh had been. He looked as young and as thin-faced and tense and fearful. Letters and cards from his classmates were tacked up on the wall, just as in Hugh's hospital room. Hugh felt his eyes water and had to turn his face aside; even as he tried to control his breathing, he thought, "This is ridiculous. I come to cheer this kid up, and I start bawling."

He asked specific questions of Giles then, and learned with amazement that the boy's core temperature had been twenty degrees lower than Hugh's when he was found. In addition to the frostbite on Giles's feet, his hands were damaged.

It was a rushed visit, as Hugh had been given a strict time limit. Every minute the two were interrupted—by nurses, the telephone, doctors. But they established a connection, sharing the loss and even a strange fame.

Giles tried to explain to Hugh how he felt, tried to get something out that he couldn't. Hugh knew what it was, though. The boy felt that he would never heal, never get better.

Leaving, Hugh doubted that he'd been of much use. He had found himself helpless to do more than nod at the message Giles had been unable to articulate. But later, an article that appeared in a local paper was headlined, "Hugh Herr Inspires Youth Crippled on Mount Hood." Giles was quoted as describing Hugh's visit as the best encouragement of his ordeal.

The next day Hugh and the Jimmersons drove north to Seattle and Index, a steep, dank cliff about an hour east of the city. There they found Todd Skinner, one of the country's leading rock climbers, working on a free ascent of the aid crack *City Park*. Hugh gave the route a few tries, then told Mike he'd have to come back after making some improvements on his crack feet; he needed to strengthen them and plane the vertical toe blade.

When Todd succeeded on *City Park*, rated 5.13-plus, it was considered a candidate for the hardest crack climb in the world. Another top U.S. climber, Alan Watts, put in a gallant effort but left after lacerating a finger on the route. Hugh's ascent followed Todd's by about a week.

In Seattle, Hugh attracted considerable attention by bouldering on the Practice Rock, a hold-studded concrete structure set up at the University of Washington. He was wearing his pipestem legs, alternating between short and long ones for the different boulder problems. For a particular problem he wore one of each.

Next he and the Jimmersons went farther north to Vancouver and an area known as Squamish. Hugh was seeking the coveted second ascent of *Zombie Roof*. He'd read that it had gone unrepeated since first done by a Canadian climber, Peter Croft, in 1982. He and Mike worked the route, with Hugh getting farther and farther out along the roof until the day he reached above the roof in pounding rain, turned sideways, and pulled through. He yelled with delight.

They went back to the parking lot and spoke with a few other climbers, who asked what they'd done. "Huey just did the second ascent of *Zombie Roof*," Mike told them proudly.

"Oh," said one. "Perry Beckham just did that last week."

Hugh was crushed. No one is ever remembered for third ascents. As they drove away, he stared at the windshield wipers. "Well, I bet he didn't do it in the rain," he said. And he laughed.

After leaving his friends in Oregon, Hugh went south and tried the

ZOMBIE ROOF, SQUAMISH, BRITISH COLUMBIA   MICHAEL JIMMERSON

5.13 *Sphinx Crack* in the South Platte, Colorado. He came close to making it up the thin, sharp fissure. He tried the route for three days, secretly hoping to beat the record of the latest French star, Patrick Edlinger, who had completed it after only eleven falls. Hugh felt sure he could do the route, so sure that each time he fell he was very surprised. He stopped only because he had to catch his prepaid flight back east.

The whole trip, he admitted to himself afterward, was really his attempt to prove he could still go out and climb the hardest routes if he wanted to. He had also, he knew, been ready for another dose of the limelight.

And although he loved *City Park* – thought it was one of the greatest routes he had ever been on – overall, the effect of the climbs on this road trip was rather flat. After *Stage Fright* Hugh had been excited that he could push himself so hard. Now, however, although he was exhilarated to find that even without training he could compare with the best climbers, it was almost too easy. The trip actually made him want to be in school all the more. It seemed even dull to be able to perform so well without much practice. He hadn't felt the emotions of *Stage Fright* or even the thrill of taking a hard exam. He did get the publicity – his picture appeared in *Climbing* magazine and the Patagonia catalogue – but that, too, seemed shallow.

———— • ————

The next summer he went to Yosemite and made a climbing film for *National Geographic* titled "Sheer Courage." He then worked for J-Rat, a climbing equipment manufacturer in Boulder. Though he was within easy reach of good cliffs, he climbed little.

He returned to Pennsylvania for the 1987 fall term. All semester there were phone calls back and forth to Julie-Anne Warll, a psychology student at the University of Colorado, whom he'd met in Boulder. Hugh decided to spend some time studying in Boulder, both because Julie-Anne was there and because he liked Boulder himself. He thought he might climb there, too, but he wasn't sure how much.

That winter he visited Julie-Anne and her parents in northern New Jersey and accompanied the Warlls on a vacation trip to Palm Beach.

One day there, he and Julie-Anne found themselves locked out of the family's rooms, seven stories up.

"I can climb up," Hugh said. Julie-Anne just looked at him. Quickly, Hugh stepped up on the railing that circled a patio. He palmed the ceiling above with one hand while he reached over and grabbed a rail on the bottom of the deck above. He heard Julie-Anne laughing. He latched onto the railing of the next deck, laybacked, and manteled up. He stood, palmed again, and reached again.

The hardest part was going fast enough that people inside wouldn't see him. "If the police come," he told Julie-Anne, "I'll be sitting on the floor with my legs off, saying, 'I don't know what you're talking about.'"

———— • ————

In January 1988 he began classes at the University of Colorado. In this area he had once fired off pitch after pitch of hard climbing, and been part of the climbing scene. Now he did little but study.

He came up with what he thought was another breakthrough: the idea of not going to class. He stayed in his rented room and studied his books, avoiding painful legwork; it saved a lot of time, too. He felt he could get more out of an hour spent alone with his books. He went to his physics class only twice that semester.

He liked the idea that now his work was not just handed to him. He had to try very hard, which he found especially satisfying. He also felt he understood things better for that. That was what he wanted, to understand.

He felt, in a way, that he was letting people down by not climbing. "Oh, you aren't?" they'd ask.

"I'd like to climb," he would say, "but when I climb, I destroy my whole body. If I continue to climb, I probably won't be able to walk when I'm forty." He sometimes missed it, but not often; he had replaced it. He knew that if he climbed at all, he would try to climb at the highest level.

One day Neil Cannon took Hugh to the hills to a bouldering area, Flagstaff, just before a big physics exam. Hugh returned to town and took the test, along with some four hundred other students. The average grade was 67, but he got a 96.

In spring Hugh and another friend, Cindy Pieropan, began going to Flagstaff with some regularity. But the bouldering was secondary. Their usual intent was to watch the evening glow as it hit the rocks and valley.

One dusk, as the two hurried out of Cindy's car to catch the fading shafts of sunshine, they saw Charlie Fowler, a career climber Hugh knew from the old days.

"What are you up to?" Charlie asked.

"Charlie, we're looking for light!" said Hugh. He saw a beam of sun strike a rock on the hillside above. "Hey, Cindy! Look at that light!"

"Let's go up there!" she exclaimed.

Charlie turned with a perplexed look on his face, but Hugh was already gone. Charlie paused, then reached for his chalk bag and headed back to the boulders.

Hugh that spring was blissful. Everything seemed poetic, romantic, full of potential. He had spent so much time inside with his books that now he was like Bilbo again, emerging from the dark forest to find the sun.

|18|

In the summer of 1988 Hugh heard bad news. Ed Webster of Boulder, a climber-photographer whom Hugh knew, had badly frostbitten his fingers and toes on Mount Everest. He and his teammates, who without carrying oxygen had forged a new route up the Kangshung Face, had barely gotten down the mountain alive. Most of his fingertips and some of his toes would have to be amputated. His fingers were the worst, as he had at one point taken off his mittens to shoot some photos.

Now Ed was home, in the care of his friends and doctors. To concerned friends who sent cards and gifts, he wrote back letters that jingled with talk of the future, his projects, his gratefulness to be alive and at home, and eating out in Mexican restaurants. Depression, however, would come later, in waves.

Said Hugh: "The elation of being alive will stay with him always. It has for me. He may be depressed, but then he'll remember, 'I'm alive!'"

———•———

A conversation Hugh had with Ron Warll crystallized into an opportunity. Hugh had told Ron that he wanted to know more about polyurethane and its possible advantages for use in prosthetics. He explained the idea of the cushioned socket.

"Fine, let's make a prototype and test the idea," Warll told him. "We can use the machinery down at the shop." Warll and his partner, Bud Kirkpatrick, owned Dicar, Inc., a production shop that made parts for the machines that punch out corrugated boxes. He invited Hugh to stay at his home for the summer.

By now Hugh and Julie-Anne were no longer dating, for the same reason as always – Hugh's intentness on his own projects, now school instead of rock climbing – but they remained good friends. Julie-Anne, in any case, was away for the summer.

Ron Warll's role was that of adviser and promoter; Bud Kirkpatrick was manufacturing consultant. Hugh could work with Warll's employees, use the shop's specialized equipment, and procure materials and samples.

Over time the idea for the device developed: it was a stump-receiving socket with several inflatable bladders, whose pressures would be regulated by the amputee. The inflatable bladders would be custom-fit flexible membranes made of polyurethane. The membranes pressing against the weight-bearing portions of the stump would provide a fairly soft, smooth surface. Sections of the stump that for anatomical considerations should not be under pressure would receive less force. The wearer could adjust his prosthesis for the daily changes in his limb. An amputee's legs usually start out swollen in the morning, and shrink during the day.

Working with Kirkpatrick and Kenny Christian, a chemical engineer at Dicar, Hugh began the process of forming the urethane bladders around the stump. Despite various modifications, the process stayed roughly the same, and he had to follow each step each time, making all new components.

Hugh's goal was to create the physical manifestation of his vision for the device. If he made a prototype that didn't match the specifications of what he had visualized, he couldn't be sure of what he was testing. If he thought, for example, that a certain bladder should be located at a particular spot, and he accidentally built it at a different spot, and that accident worked, he wouldn't know why it had succeeded

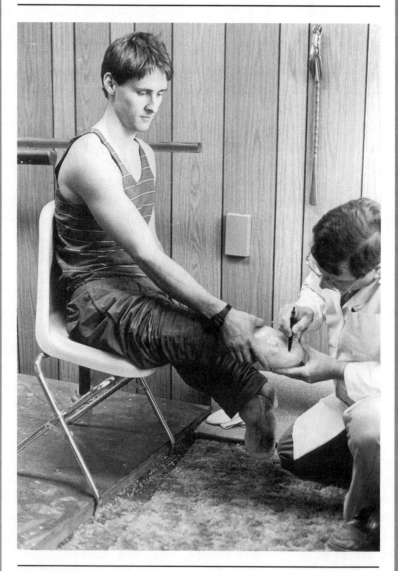

MECHANICSBURG, PENNSYLVANIA   HH

and wouldn't be able to replicate it. The whole game was, through creating and testing physical models, to solve the problems of fluid socket design.

Work on every prototype began at Gosthnian's office in Pennsylvania. Hugh would then spend as long as two weeks in New Jersey, at Dicar, before returning to Pennsylvania for the two days it took to attach the shank. He would walk around on the leg, redesign it, and begin making an improved version.

To build a typical prototype, he would make a cast of his own stump. When the material stiffened, he would pop the cast off and fill that cup with molding material. At first he used plaster of paris, but that retained moisture, which created problems when the plug was later heated, so he changed to a urethane called Reprocast. The resulting plug was an accurate model of his own stump. He spread a uniform quarter-inch of wax over it.

Then he laminated his cup-shaped carbon-fiber shell, which would become the outside of the artificial limb, with acrylic resin. Into the carbon-fiber wall he laminated valve plates, one for each of the bladders, and cured the resin in a vacuum. Later, the valve plates would be drilled and tapped, and he would screw valves into the holes so that fluid could be injected into the bladders.

He would turn from the shell back to the plug. The volume of the quarter-inch wax buildup on the plug surface represented two things. The eighth of an inch of wax closest to the plug would be an inner layer of urethane; the outer layer would be empty space. Punctuating the space, however, would be divisions between the bladders, where the inner urethane sock would be bonded to the inside surface of the carbon-fiber shell.

He made and placed a jig, or brace, to ensure the critical, correct placement of the shell and plug once the wax was removed. He next bolted the entire apparatus to a metal plate, which contained holes. He melted out the wax, unscrewed the brace, and lifted the shell from the plug.

Against the inside surface of the shell he inserted eighth-inch spacers made of high-temperature wax, which would not melt in the oven. Then he positioned the shell, holding it above the plug, and screwed on the brace.

He placed a second Reprocast mold around the outside of the carbon-fiber shell where it touched the metal plate to keep the liquid urethane from oozing out. The next step was to make vents of plastic tubes and insert them between the outer surface of the shell and the second Reprocast mold. The tube ends would be held high in the air so that the urethane couldn't escape.

He poured in the urethane. For the five minutes before it jelled, the mold was placed on a vibrating table to make air bubbles rise. The bubbles would pass through the plastic tubes and out of the mold, reach the surface, and break.

He cured the assembly for eighteen hours at 250 degrees Fahrenheit. Then he bonded the urethane along the divisions, using adhesives. He drilled and tapped the plates and screwed in the valves. Finally, with shank and foot attached, the socket was ready for Hugh to test.

Hugh couldn't wait to walk on the first leg fitted with the new socket. Barry Gosthnian looked out his door to see Hugh strolling around the office building. The next time he looked, he saw Hugh lying in a bush like a drunken sailor. The glue joint between the leg's shank and socket had snapped.

Gosthnian said, as he picked Hugh up and brushed him off, "What the hell were you doing walking on it? The glue's not cured yet."

"I learn a little more from every one," Hugh said wearily.

———— • ————

At first he tried several kinds of urethane. An elastomer, urethane ranges in hardness from something resembling Jell-O to something like aluminum. Hugh could arrive at different properties by using various backbones of esters and ethers.

Early on, he learned the hard way how readily urethane can generate foam if the molds retain moisture. It was on a day when he thought he had followed directions precisely: he kept the material under a nitrogen blanket, he degassed it after mixing, he had the mixture at the right temperature, he poured it into the right-temperature mold, and he put it in the right-temperature oven. But the material bubbled and foamed as it reacted. That was the incident that caused Hugh and his co-workers to abandon the use of the porous plaster plug and switch to the hard, nonporous material Reprocast.

He also had to experiment with different adhesives for bonding the urethane sleeve to the shell. He wanted to make the sleeve replaceable so that a leaky bladder could be readily fixed. He tried one adhesive after another, each time scraping it off and starting from scratch. He wore one leg for three weeks before it sprang a leak. On the next prototype he tried yet another new adhesive for bonding the divisions.

Once Hugh used wax as a release agent to keep the urethane from adhering to the plug after curing. The wax didn't work, and when he removed his materials from the oven, he couldn't pull the urethane off the plug. He had to sit with a hammer in hand, chipping the hard plug out of the urethane sock.

Another time a machinist, bolting the plug onto the plate by drilling from underneath, drilled too far. The drill poked through the outer surface of the plug. When Hugh poured the urethane in, it ran through the tunnel in the plug and out the holes in the bottom of the metal plate, into a puddle on the floor.

He also learned about false economics when, to save money, he bought lower-temperature wax. Although Hugh and the others swabbed the outer surfaces of two PVA bags (used in the lamination process to trap the liquid resin as it flows along the outer surface of the plug) with acetone for an hour to keep the heat down, the wax deformed under the high temperatures that result when the acrylic resin cures. The distance between the plug and the carbon fiber was no longer a quarter of an inch, and the mold was ruined. Because Hugh had used this wax to save $50, Dicar and Barry Gosthnian had lost $200 worth of urethane, $20 in carbon fiber, and $15 in resin – and Hugh had lost a week and a half of effort.

Working with urethane was as much an art as a science. Sometimes Hugh would process the urethane just as standards dictated, then look at it and say, "It should be doing something else, but it isn't." He learned how to clean urethane parts, how to prepare them, how to bond urethane, and what kinds of chemicals to use. He learned that he must make the cast of his leg – his own stump – under pressure, as if it were being walked on, by using a hydrostatic pressure chamber.

He studied the forces to be applied. Because of anatomical constraints, some areas of the stump are sensitive to high external pressures; others are able to withstand them. These different pressure zones across the stump surface dictated the placement of the fluid bladders. He would have to divide the pressures. The back of the leg–muscle tissue–could take a lot of pressure. The side–the bursa and tendons–could take far less.

Sometimes he and the Dicar specialists kicked around ideas and dismissed them, then came back to them. Sometimes the other workers had to calm the anxious Hugh down.

The first prototype weighed twenty pounds. The seventeenth weighed one pound.

At the end of a long day in the lab, Hugh had to ask Dave Finnegan, another employee, to help him carry his things out to his car. "My knees and my legs are hurting more and more," he told Dave. "I get less and less mobile, less independent. This project is about my survival."

One day it occurred to Bob Longendyck, vice president of manufacturing at Dicar, that Hugh didn't appear to be keeping lab reports. "Hugh, are you writing all of this down in a manual?" Bob asked.

"Are you kidding? I would never forget any of these things," said Hugh. "This project is too important. I could destroy my knees forever if I forgot things. I won't forget."

———— • ————

"In climbing," thought Hugh, "the only thing you're creating is your sequence. In this you're creating everything." He was thinking about the socket all the time.

Hugh found it one of the most frustrating endeavors he had ever taken part in. There seemed to be a million variables, a million things that could and did go wrong. He could change the type of fluid or the volume in one of the bladders and radically change everything; he could put himself on the wrong track and not know it, and then get farther away from the goal than ever.

But he learned from his frustrations. He learned to step back and take a second look, and not to dismiss anything as foolish or inappropriate. He applied the same intensity he had used to climb *Super Crack* and stuck with the project. No one ever heard him say, "That's it."

When Kenny Christian was ready to leave for home at the end of a day, Hugh often called him back, pleading, "Come on, cast one more part for me." Other times, discouraged by some aspect of the process, Hugh would say, "Would you just get a gun and shoot me right now? Please, Kenny?"

During the anxious times, he liked being in the lab. He found that having the other people around him gave him confidence.

19

Rather than interrupt his work on the project, Hugh took time off from his studies in the fall of 1988 to refine the socket. From May to November that year Hugh and Barry Gosthnian made two or three prototypes a month, totaling in the end seventeen. At every change he recommended for the next prototype, Hugh was nervous – it could be either an improvement or a disaster.

Gosthnian himself got caught up in the excitement. After dinner he sometimes disappeared into the machine shop next door and stayed until one or two in the morning. He knew that great advances were being made in the field, especially in materials. On their better days, he and Hugh felt they were part of a new wave, on the verge of a new era of hope and mobility for amputees. But their attitudes swung from delight to, "Oh my God, what did we do? Are we sure we want to do this? Why did we ever start?"

"He is relentless," Gosthnian said to his wife, Linda, one night. "When he gets excited, it's like sharks in a feeding frenzy." Their sessions usually ended with Barry saying, "Give it a try, Hugh. Get it walking, and let me know what you've got." Hugh was often in the field, determining how well his assembly worked and how long its components lasted. There were usually half a dozen prototypes in his car trunk at a given time.

For the field research, he was irreplaceable. Engineering numbers were available on the different aspects of urethane. What such a project as the socket needed was field testing, but it couldn't be done by just any amputee. Most people don't have the analytical skills to say what's wrong when something hurts, and an amputee's pain may not be direct but referred, emanating from one source but feeling as though it comes from another. Sometimes Hugh felt tendon pain the day after wearing a new leg, caused by incorrect pressure. The testing process was risky – he could hurt himself permanently.

From the Dicar lab he often called Gosthnian three or four times a day, and sometimes more. Although he liked the sense of support he felt in the lab, working alongside dedicated people, Hugh often slipped into his own world and wouldn't speak for hours on end. He was again reminded of himself as a climber, both before and after the accident. Then, too, he had been wholly immersed in his pursuit of perfection, overwhelmed by it.

At Dicar, as on a difficult route, he gave the project his all. He didn't care whether he would have anything left for the next day. He didn't think about anything but the problems and the goal. He couldn't imagine a world in which the goal was not his only focus.

But there was one difference. Except for his bout with tendinitis, and the time in the Littleton hospital, when he'd put all expectations on hold, he had never before thought there was anything he couldn't do. Now, though, he prepared himself by saying, "This might not work."

———— • ————

Hugh was now back in touch with Jeff Batzer. Jeff had enrolled in a seminary and hoped to become a minister. They discussed school and spiritual matters and science. One night Hugh asked whether Jeff would have gone into the ministry if not for the accident.

"It's because of that that I am where I am today," said Jeff, "although I think God could have found other ways."

"If the accident had never happened," said Hugh, "I would still be a mindless jock."

SPHINX CRACK, SOUTH PLATTE, COLORADO   JOHN SHERMAN

———— • ————

Hugh needed to determine where the bladders should be positioned around the stump to achieve the proper force distribution. He would have to consider anatomical factors and the stump dynamics during basic motions: piston actions, for example, and knee-toe rotations.

"I don't think it's ever the kind of thing that's here and done," said Bob Longendyck at Dicar.

"What's 'done'?" asked Hugh rhetorically, agreeing. "Is it done if most amputees in the country are wearing it?"

"Two things would happen then. Problems will start coming back. Thousands of people will give input. Then a guy who knows something says, 'I can do it better.'

"In industry," Bob continued, "you can never say, 'I've got it now.'"

———— • ————

In the winter, early in 1989, Hugh returned to Millersville and switched his major to physics.

"I am not very smart, but I can learn, and learn very difficult things," he reflected. "It's a matter of application and effort. I am able to understand things, but it's not there immediately. I seem to be good at everything but not great at anything.

"But I know what it means to focus, to transform a complex world into its true essence, dissolving the details. The abstract, pure essence: what makes something work."

Through his new major he met students who shared his interests, and he began socializing.

He split the summer between New Jersey and Pennsylvania, working again with Dicar and Barry Gosthnian. Before school began in fall 1989 he took a trip to see Tony, now living in Aspen, Colorado, and working a carpentry job. Elaine now happened to be living in Aspen as well.

The three went climbing together in Independence Pass. The granite was steep, gray-gold, dotted with lumpy flakes and bulbous holds. In the valley below them, a stand of aspens glinted soft green in the light. Nearer, scrub oak and dark olive pine stretched up the opposite side of the pass in wide lines, interspersed with sweeps of dry brown grass.

After a few pitches, the three lounged in the sun. Hugh spoke of his tendon problems, and his prospects. "If I suddenly had to be in a wheelchair, I could cope with it," he said calmly. "I'm a chameleon. I could easily change my life."

He wondered as he spoke whether he had been that way as an adolescent or had become that way after the accident. He didn't know because he had never been forced to make any real adjustments prior to age seventeen. Maybe he could say so only now that he had learned of the life of the mind. "There's so much you can do," he thought.

"If tomorrow I were confined to a wheelchair," he continued out loud, "I could see myself in a short time becoming a professor, and perfectly content, because my outlet would be study. It really wouldn't be much different, except socially. Actually, it would be quite comfortable."

Later, as the three coiled their ropes and sorted carabiners and hardware, he mentioned that he was reading the Bible again, from a philosophical as much as a religious point of view.

"Listen to some of the lines in the Bible," he said. "'Blessed are those who believe without seeing'—isn't that incredible? People who believe without seeing create new ideas and mechanisms. They are blessed, they are given the power of creation.

"Believing's the only way I can keep working on the limb socket. That was part of climbing, too. It's magic, when you dream of something and then do it."

"Do you believe in God?" Elaine asked.

"Look at how structured and how beautifully put together nature is," Hugh answered.

"Is that what convinces you?"

"Partly." Through studying physics in school, he said, he had begun seeing science as part of his world. "The universe is not inscrutable. It's all completely comprehendible. I even think that life after death can be understood by the human intellect.

"In the end science and religion and everything will bleed into one. There'll be a *unified* unified theory. It will explain things we don't understand, such as clairvoyance. There is magic, but someday, with the expansion of the mind, human beings will understand all things."

He had taken a new interest in the outside world, in the destruction of rain forests in Brazil and the effects on animals and ice caps. "We as individuals are very intelligent," he lectured, "but as a group we're idiots."

The two brothers talked about women. Tony had just ended a long-term relationship and wanted to meet someone else. Hugh thought that his brother seemed more like his old self than he had in years: wanting to be around people, to climb, to take some college courses. "There isn't that angry edge to him anymore," he thought.

Hugh himself was looking for something new and different; he thought he was ready for a relationship on a different plane. "I'd like to share," he said. "I haven't found anyone that I can share with. Most of the women I've been with, it's been limited. The relationships are just male-female."

He had a long talk with Elaine before he left, over tea at her kitchen table, where the window looked out toward Independence Pass. The front lawn was splotched with patches of scorched straw-yellow.

"Part of being an athlete was being accepted, admired," he said. "So why do I sit for six months reading? Yes, I love it. I must be doing it for more than acceptance, but that's at least part of it. I like pushing things to the limit, I like to feel I'm contributing, but I also think that's hooked into being accepted and admired. To be loved by strangers—that's a fabulous idea . . .

"But part of making this socket was recognizing what was wrong with myself, what my fears were," he said. "I've found that as soon as I get arrogant, I fall short of my expectations.

"I don't think I'm going to succeed unless I'm doing it for the right reasons, independent of money and fame, not wanting the credit. I should be in the frame of mind where I'd be doing it even if it meant never having my name on it."

———————— • ————————

On May 8, 1990, Hugh Herr and Barry Gosthnian received United States Patent number 4,923,475 for their completed socket.

20

In New Hampshire one early-winter day, Rob Walker, an International Mountain Equipment employee, and his friend Matt Peer walked six miles off the road to Mount Bartlett, in the White Mountains. It was thirty degrees and snowing. For a warm-up they decided to solo the first forty feet of their intended ice climb and then sit on a ledge to uncoil their rope and begin belaying each other.

They were both fit. Rob had run a marathon three weeks before. He had been running a great deal lately, but it hadn't occurred to him that he could be anemic and weakened.

He climbed easily to the ledge and sank both axes into the ice above it. As he fell, the last thing he saw before losing consciousness was the axes in the wall.

He came to on the ground. "I'll go for help," Matt said. Rob was wearing a cotton turtleneck, long underwear, and wool knickers. Matt dug into a pack for a sweater, then tried to give him a Gore-Tex shell, but Rob did not dare sit up to put it on: he could tell there was something wrong with his back. "I'll be back soon," said Matt.

Alone, Rob waited four hours. He wiggled his toes. He knew he might lose some to frostbite. The temperatures weren't extreme, but he wasn't warmly dressed.

Bill Kane and David Stone of Mountain Rescue ran the six miles from the highway to Mount Bartlett in their sneakers. It took two hours for rescuers to place Rob on a litter and six hours to carry him to safety.

Rob escaped more easily than he had expected, with three compressed vertebrae, and a broken collarbone and ankle. During the time alone in the snow and while he was being carried, he kept thinking of Hugh. "Look what happened to him," he thought. "And he's all right."

———— • ————

Lynn Hill was on a winning streak. In the new World Cup competition tour, climbers ascended courses on man-made indoor walls studded with fiberglass holds. The carefully rigged moves became increasingly harder the higher the climbers got, and climbers were scored according to the highest handhold attained. In the three years since these contests' inception, Hill had won nine of the twelve World Cup events she had entered.

Now she was climbing in France with Russ Raffa when she got to the top of a pitch, clipped her rope through some eye-ring bolts at the top, leaned back – and began falling through the air. Her rope, which somehow had not been tied, had whipped out of her harness. She shouted her husband's name. Then she screamed.

She waved her arms to keep from turning over backward, then covered her head, curled into a ball, and did a tuck dive toward the treetops.

For Raffa, watching, it was as if his world had suddenly gone into slow motion, as if he were taking photos, observing. Snap one, snap two, snap three. He wanted to take away the moment, be somewhere else, have this not be happening. His eyes met Lynn's.

She slammed into a tree with the left side of her body and spun to the right as she hit the ground. She landed between two car-sized boulders, in a dirt patch a few feet wide. She just missed a stump.

On the ground, she went immediately into shock. Raffa tried to talk to her and cleaned out her dirt-filled eyes. She mumbled questions,

John Herr and his sons had traversed thirty miles in Canada, from a glacier in the remote Selkirk Mountains clear to Banff, on a trail that was five thousand to nine thousand feet in elevation. They had passed Moraine Lake into British Columbia, looked down onto turquoise Lake O'Hara and the lighter, bird's-egg-blue Lake Oesa, and ended up at a teahouse at Lake Louise eating blueberry pie and drinking lemonade. Hugh was eight years old, and embarrassed.

He had lost his balance in a boulder field that day, and fallen head-first between two boulders. Wedged in upside-down, his feet waving in the air, he had been unable to extricate himself. His father, realizing that the boy was unhurt, laughed long and hard.

But Hugh was thinking, "Mountains are serious."

asking where she was and what had happened. A friend, Jennifer Cole, ran for help. Hill came to, groggily, just before being winched up into a rescue helicopter. She had broken a bone in her foot, dislocated her elbow, and received punctures in her shoulder and chest. She needed stitches in her shoulder and nose, and under her chin.

Hill had been tying her rope into her harness when she noticed her shoes were out of reach. She got up to retrieve them, put them on, and didn't think again about the knot. The day was cold; Hill's bulky jacket covered the harness loops where her rope was threaded but not tied. She never noticed.

One day after he heard about Hill's accident, Hugh was with someone who said, "What a stupid bitch. How could she have done something so dumb?"

Hugh said to him evenly, "It could happen to anyone. What she did was just a mistake."

Lynn Hill phoned him one night and said, "Hugh, both of us didn't think of something we should have. We're both on our second lives."

They talked on, and Hugh told her about his work on the socket.

"Maybe there's a reason we lived," she said. "Hugh, I think your reason is being expressed right now." She asked him how he felt whenever news of other accidents filtered back.

"It might be sick," he said, "but hearing about things like your fall— it makes me feel better." It was as if the two, and other climbers who had suffered accidents, were all part of a strange club, sharing a camaraderie of near-misses and sadness, and perhaps a fellowship of errors and culpability as well.

———— • ————

Kevin Bein, a longtime Shawangunks climber, died in a fall on the Matterhorn. Elaine and Hugh went to the Gunks for a memorial service. They met at a restaurant, the Northern Lights. Shaken and raw, they veered into talking of painful things. They continued their talk in the car, in the parking lot, before starting up the engine to go see Kevin's wife, Barbara. The conversation shifted to Hugh's accident.

"Did you ever think of going to see the Dows?"

"No. That would bring back a lot of bad feelings for them. And me."

"Maybe they'd like to know what you're doing, learn that the person their son"—she couldn't say it—"was looking for turned out to be a good person."

"I'd be afraid to. What would be the purpose?"

"If they knew you were a productive human being . . . if they knew you went and visited that kid from Mount Hood, got straight As in school, were making artificial limbs—maybe they'd like that."

"But is it my place to tell them what I'm up to? What rights do I have?" In North Conway he had had no right to judge, to be like anyone else, or—some thought—even to be in that town. He had, he thought, no right to remind the Dows of his existence.

"Is it resolved now?"

"No. There's shame."

"Do you think you'll ever get rid of it?"

"Probably not." She saw, by the light of the Northern Lights' sign, that a tear had tracked down his face.

"From everything I've heard about Albert, he would not want you to torture yourself about it."

"I'm sure," he said.

"I do think that he would want you to accept it, and go on and be a happy person, and not suffer forever."

There was a long silence. "I always think that when I die, I'll see Albert," he said.

It was late when Hugh and Elaine arrived at the apartment Barbara and Kevin had shared for more than a decade, and the three just said their good-nights. But the next night Elaine and Hugh asked Barbara to come out and sleep on mattresses in the living room with them, to camp out.

She hesitated. She had a perfectly good bed in the next room. "Well, O.K.," she said, smiling.

All three lay on their pads, in their sleeping bags. Elaine asked the others to play a sort of game, to list five things that meant self-identification to them. They could use adjectives, nouns, any word at all.

Barbara faltered, and Elaine asked if maybe she'd instead like to name Kevin's list. Barbara again thought for a while and then said that the word that really came into her mind was *bridge*. Kevin, the warm-hearted, vital core of the Gunks, had been like a lighted bridge between people.

Then Elaine asked Hugh to give his list.

"Dreams, light, obsession, future, pain, faith." Hugh reeled the words off without hesitation, adding a sixth. His terms were all abstract.

"Can I have another one?" he asked.

"Sure."

"Visionary." He added a few more: "Always running. Never satisfied."

"What if you had to name just one?" Elaine suggested.

Again without pause, he said, naming the title of a song by the Police, "King of Pain."

"Why do you say that?"

He didn't use the first person in his answer. "So overloaded, couldn't take anything else," he said.

The next day, he and Elaine went climbing. Barbara hadn't wanted to; she had seen Kevin fall—a rock had broken off as he prepared to rappel from it—and could not imagine ever wanting to climb again.

Though he had barely climbed in months and lacked endurance, Hugh still had power. He managed two 5.12s, including a toprope repeat of *Super Crack*.

Afterward the two sat at a picnic table outside a convenience store for a lunch of water, bananas, and yogurt. They spoke of other climbing accidents, and Hugh said that only now, all these years later, did he dare ever make judgments—whether about climbing or mountaineering or anything else.

"It's only in the last year or so that I've really let down my hair," he added. "Until one year ago, whenever I took my legs off at home, I wouldn't take my socks off. I would get in bed and then take the socks off. I didn't want to look. I didn't even know I was doing that—it took a friend to point it out to me. Late, by night, I'm vulnerable, emotional, tired. That's when I cry."

"Do you still cry much?"

"Sometimes. It's a great release. I cried just a week ago."

"Over what?"

"Over Kevin Bein"—he paused and gave a half-chuckle—"and a socket prototype."

There was a silence. "Why aren't you climbing anymore? You have so much talent, it just seems like you should use it," she said, voice trailing off.

"I don't have to climb to use my talent. I'm not obsessed about the actual sport of climbing. I'm obsessed about being inspired. It could be anything—a lot of things inspire me. I have to be up against the wall to feel good about myself.

"It would be so irrational for me to climb," he continued. "I'm very fragile physically. Climbing just tears me up. It hurts like hell. It's mostly the walking, but the climbing gets my shoulders and arms, too. If I write for an hour now, my tendons flare. I already have to wear an orthopedic mitt to write, because of tendon problems from climbing."

"What's the role of the climbing community in your life now?" This was his first trip to the Gunks in about two years.

"You know," he said, "I just switch off from people. I can be with people, then go do something else for months. It doesn't mean I'm sick of them. I was here at the Gunks for so long, and then left. I had no problem with that. When I come back, though, I'm glad to be here.

"My friends are who I'm with. I float around. I don't necessarily keep in touch, even with someone I consider a very close friend. A memory of a place or person lasts. I don't have to be in contact with a friend to love him. People who don't understand that can get offended."

"Are you as happy a person as you were when you were here before?"

"I'm a happier person now than I was as a kid, and I was a happy kid. My feelings of happiness are much more profound. In the same way that the world is more wonderful if you've been shut indoors, happiness is more acute if you've been unhappy. There's a profound relief.

"Out of adversity came the realization that adversity is not all bad. I don't like looking at the past—it brings back the pain of that stage—but I'm a deeper person for it.

"If it wasn't for Albert Dow, I would never regret it. If it wasn't for him, I'd do it all again."

"The accident?" She was incredulous. "Losing your legs?"

He nodded, not asking her to believe but willing to explain. "I've learned a lot. With my insights, I have a lot to give the world. I mean that. I've thought about it a lot. I don't know where it'll all surface.

"Whether Albert Dow's death is on my hands or the hands of an omnipotent God will always be unclear to me. Albert's body is gone, but the memory of Albert is pushing me, maybe toward the completion of some unforeseeable design – something I was meant to do in my life."

21

How much did it really help now, Hugh asked himself, to think, "At least I'm alive"? He decided that his happiness was not due to that alone. At seventeen he hadn't had many ties to the world, just to his family. He'd had no sense that he was important, that he should stick around. Only in the last few years had he begun to respect himself and his role. And it had nothing to do with climbing.

These days, he never dreamed about having feet. He sometimes wondered what it would be like to have them, though, just for one day—to compare his artificial feet with human feet. His was not a sad longing.

He began climbing again, on weekends, with some regularity. He climbed for pleasure and for the camaraderie. Now he mostly thought of climbing in terms that could perhaps be described as grateful. It had taught him at a young age the virtues of having goals, taught him how to concentrate.

His new goals were to find an end to pain and to see a day when people were not handicapped, because technology had freed them. He was searching, aiming for something, reaching. He couldn't have said where he was going to end up, but he knew he was progressing to greater skills and a higher happiness.

———— • ————

As he finished his final term at Millersville, Hugh had gotten only one B, in Intro to Film. His grade-point average in science was 4.0.

Awards and recognition streamed in. The university honored him with a plaque and a resolution. He stood up and made a speech of thanks. "Today was a very proud day for the Herr family," said his father afterward.

Then he received the Young American Award from the Boy Scouts of America: three days' worth of awards and ceremonies, and a check for $5,000. He wore his only suit and made several speeches.

He gave a talk at the Central Pennsylvania Annual Physics Convention, attended by professors and students. The lecture was titled, "The Static Equilibrium Conditions of the Lower Extremity Fluid Prosthetic Socket and the Supported Biological Limb."

He was a guest-speaker at a state conference for the organization known as SADD, Student Athletes who Detest Drugs.

He was voted into the Pennsylvania Sports Hall of Fame.

A Channel 9 news segment in New York City featuring him won a local Emmy; because he had been involved in the editing, he, too, was included in the Emmy. He added the certificate to the other awards on his wall.

USA Today, the national newspaper, named him for its All-U.S.A. College Academic Team along with only nineteen other students in the nation. The newspaper ran an article on each and gave them all checks for $2,500. Wrote *Climbing* magazine, referring to the country's newly formed competitive climbing team, "Eight years ago, if a U.S. Climbing Team had existed, Hugh Herr would have been on it. Instead, he's part of the U.S. Academic Team."

A reporter-photographer from the local newspaper came to his house. Hugh was downstairs in his room in the basement when his mother opened the door at the top of the stairway.

"Hugh, the photographer's here!" she called down. Hugh grunted an acknowledgment. His mother took two steps downstairs. In a whis-

ROCKS STATE PARK, MARYLAND   HH

per she added, "And she's *gorgeous!*" Hugh walked up from the basement to the porch as Lee Blithe, carrying a spiral notebook and a camera, stepped into his life. It was the afternoon of January 26, 1990, exactly eight years after Hugh was rescued on Mount Washington.

———— • ————

That spring Hugh applied to three graduate schools. He visited the University of Colorado and spoke with Igor Gamow, a chemical engineering professor and inventor. Du Pont had distributed his Gamow Bag, a portable airtight container used to treat victims of high-altitude sickness by creating the air pressure of low altitude.

As they toured the engineering facility, Gamow showed Hugh his latest idea. It was a giant flipper, with two foils like those on airplane wings, that could propel a person through water at high speed. But the way Gamow was attaching the apparatus to his leg, using blocks and screws, it looked to Hugh like a medieval torture device.

Hugh immediately envisioned a proper orthotic brace. He made a flexible plastic mold of Gamow's leg and built front and back shin guards. He bolted the front guard to the wing and added Velcro straps so that the wearer could cinch himself in. The first day it was ready, Gamow wore the prototype around his office all day. He was delighted with it.

Hugh and Gamow discussed possible designs for spring-loaded artificial limbs to be used for running. Hugh was fascinated by the project.

He was accepted at the universities of Colorado and Pennsylvania. Then a call came from Professor Robert Mann of the Massachusetts Institute of Technology. "You know you've been accepted, right?" said Mann.

Hugh was momentarily confused and dazed. He hadn't known.

"I'm going to send you some information about what we're doing here, so you can make your decision," Mann said.

The acceptance letter arrived the following day. The normal time for such a letter to go out would have been January. This was three months early, in October.

Woodie Flowers, a professor of mechanical engineering at MIT, called. "So are you really this good?" he asked.

Again caught off guard, Hugh said, "Yes." As soon as he said it, he was afraid he'd sounded arrogant.

Flowers told Hugh that he'd been doing prosthetic research for several years. At the moment one of his graduate students was working on creating a knee for an above-knee amputee, with a built-in computer that would alter resistance in the knee as the person walked. The department was interested in Hugh's ideas for the next steps toward production of the limb socket. Flowers invited Hugh to visit.

He toured the Eric P. and Evelyn E. Newman Laboratory for Biomechanics and Human Rehabilitation and spoke with MIT students about their projects and classes. He looked through their textbooks— on fluid mechanics, dynamics, control theory, and the mechanics of materials—and felt confident that he could do the work. He and Flowers discussed possibilities for the prosthetic socket. A computer weighing less than a pound could be placed within a prosthetic leg to monitor the pressure in each bladder. The system would adjust the pressures around the stump, keeping the non-weight-bearing distributions constant.

"This project will be hard, difficult enough to be your Ph.D. project," said Flowers.

Hugh returned home and phoned Don Eidam, his Millersville adviser, himself an MIT graduate.

"No shit!" said Don. "Now I can sleep."

Hugh sent his letter of acceptance to MIT that day. The spring-loaded running foot could wait. Hugh intended to get back to that some day—he still had it in his mind to run a marathon. Limitations, he knew, were illusions.

EPILOGUE

Marjorie and Albert Dow, corres-
ponding with the author of this book, wrote several kind, pained
letters.

"Our son was known as a bright, handsome, compassionate young
man. He would *never* want anyone to hurt another. He could not bear
it. Thus, the first order is for the living to be able to get on with their
lives," wrote Marjorie Dow.

"It is difficult and awkward to try to describe to you something no
one has asked us about. No one has asked us to participate in anything,
except to approve and bless the scholarship fund undertaking [in their
son's name]."

Mrs. Dow continued that people often shied away from asking
about her feelings. "They want to spare added pain," she said.

". . . We remain interested in your book and in your efforts. We
watch and listen for names and progress of those we heard [Albert]
mention or of those we met through him.

"News of Hugh's achievements was appreciated. What of the other
young man? I hope each can go on and be a contributor to society. We
wish both the best."

She described a recent drive to see the autumn foliage and wrote of sitting and looking up at "Al's mountains."

"Seeing Al's friends' children is very painful," the letter continued. "We . . . know we can never see his.

"We have lots of good memories, thank God.

"Yes, it is nearing the anniversary. We will be flying from Florida to California that day. We find it hard to be here, particularly if it is storming."

She wrote that Albert's sisters, Susan and Caryl, wished that this account of their brother would stress that he had always been willing to assist at rescues and searches. He had felt it his duty to other climbers and outdoorspeople, his community.

Marjorie Dow closed one letter by describing a rescue. Only a few days before his death, Albert had joined a difficult search for a man who, although a veteran Thiokol snowcat driver, had become separated from his vehicle. Sweeping the mountain in a wild storm, all the rescuers were tied to one another for safety. Even so, the weather prevented communication between people who were only an arm's length apart.

Albert told his mother afterward that he had thought the search was hopeless, that only by falling over the man would the searchers have found him. (In fact, the man managed to make his way to safety alone.)

Anxious for her son's safety, she asked why he had even gone. "No hesitation on Al's part as he responded, 'Mom, if I was in trouble, I would want to know someone was looking for me.' And he went out again, a few days later."

Jeff Batzer was married on January 16, 1988, six years after the accident. He would graduate in spring of 1992 from the Lancaster Bible College.

Martha and John Herr remain in Lancaster County. Ellen works as an economist in Washington, D.C. Beth married Don Gallagher, one of the brothers' climbing partners, with whom she has had three children. Tony lives near Aspen and continues to work as a building contractor. Hans was married in February 1990, with Tony and Hugh at the altar as best men beside him.

ACKNOWLEDGMENTS

In 1987 Julie and Michael Kennedy, co-owners of *Climbing* magazine, were in the latter stages of putting together a special women's issue when she got an idea.

"We really should have a profile of Barbara Washburn in this issue," Julie urged. Forty years before, Mrs. Washburn had been the first woman up Mount McKinley, making the mountain's fourth ascent.

At the time, I was living and working in Boston. "Julie, I *can't* call Alison this late and ask her to do it," Michael said.

"Then I will!" said Julie.

She telephoned me at my apartment. As it happened, I was able to take on the assignment, and set up the interviews.

Sally Atwater of Stackpole Books read the resultant article and wrote asking whether I would consider writing a book. I sent her a query for a biography of Hugh Herr. I am grateful; she has brought her tact, judgment, and skill to bear on everything that followed.

I'd like to acknowledge help and information from the Mount Washington Rescue Report: January 23–26, 1982, by Jean-Paul LeBlanc, Emergency Medical Services of New Hampshire; Joel White at the Mount Washington Weather Station; and from *Climbing, Mountain,*

Rock & Ice, and *Outside* magazines, the *Sunday Journal Magazine* of the *Providence Journal*, and the book *Fifty Classic Climbs*.

Parts of this book have appeared in the *Washington Post Magazine* and in *The Price of Adventure*, an anthology of mountain rescues.

Thanks to the Herr family for its honesty and hospitality; and especially to Tony, my neighbor and climbing pal in Colorado, for our long talks on those long Friday and Sunday night drives to and from the San Luis Valley, Canon City, and Boulder. And, of course, a benediction to Hugh, the subject, heart and soul of this book, for his forthrightness and candor; thank you, quiet Hugh, for talking.

Thanks to the Dow family, for sharing; in particular, to Marjorie Dow, for each gracious, powerful letter she sent me.

Thanks to all the people who have contributed information and photographs, and in particular to Misha Kirk, Bill Kane, and Michael Kennedy, who have read and assessed sections of the draft.

Thanks to the infinitely generous Rick and Brenda Wilcox, in whose house I lived while doing part of the research for this book.

Thanks to Bil Dunaway, publisher of the *Aspen Times*, whose offices are near my home: out of kindness and a sense of fellowship to other climbers, he let me use desk space at night and on weekends to carry out this project. Anyone with any idea of the cost of office space in Aspen will understand the size of this boon.

Thanks to Michael Benge, managing editor of *Climbing*, for his tolerant support – including the loan of his very truck when I rolled and totaled mine in a blizzard – during the vicissitudes accompanying this book's final preparations. (The first thing I handed up through the broken window when a passing motorist stopped to help me was the manuscript of *Second Ascent*.)

Thanks, finally, to my mother, Nancy Watkins Osius, for marking up this manuscript, as she has my writings for over two decades; and to my father, Ted Osius, for taking me outside in the first place.

ALISON KEITH OSIUS